THE ART OF
LIVING

THE ART OF
LIVING

Peace and Freedom in the Here and Now

———

THICH NHAT HANH

HarperOne
An Imprint of HarperCollinsPublishers

HarperCollins books may be purchased for educational, business, or sales promotional use. For information, please email the Special Markets Department at SPsales@harpercollins.com.

FIRST HARPERCOLLINS PAPERBACK PUBLISHED IN 2023

Designed by Yvonne Chan

Library of Congress Cataloging-in-Publication Data is available upon request.

ISBN 978-0-06-327648-2

23 24 25 26 27 LBC 7 6 5 4 3

CONTENTS

I first heard Thich Nhat Hanh teach in 1959 at the Xa Loi Temple in Saigon. I was a university student, full of questions about life and Buddhism. Although he was a young monk, he was already a renowned poet and accomplished scholar. That first lecture deeply impressed me. I had never heard anyone speak so beautifully and profoundly. I was struck by his learning, his wisdom, and his vision for a very practical Buddhism, deeply rooted in ancient teachings yet relevant to the needs of our time. I was already actively engaged in social work in the slums and dreamed of relieving poverty and fostering social change. Not everyone supported my dream, but "Thay" (as we liked to call Thich Nhat Hanh—the fond Vietnamese term for "Teacher") was very encouraging. He told me that he was sure anyone could touch awakening in whatever work he or she enjoyed the most. The most important thing, he said, is to just be ourselves and live our lives as deeply and mindfully as we can. I knew I had found the teacher I was looking for.

Over the last fifty-five years, I have had the privilege of study-ing and working with Thich Nhat Hanh, organizing social work programs in Vietnam, conducting peace work in Paris, rescuing boat people from the high seas, and helping him establish mindful-ness practice centers in Europe, the US, and Asia. I have witnessed Thay's teachings evolve and deepen, adapting to the ever-changing needs and challenges of our times. He has always eagerly engaged in dialogue with leaders in science, health, politics, education, business, and technology, so he can deepen his understanding of our current situation and develop mindfulness practices that are appropriate and effective. Right up to his unexpected stroke in November 2014, at the age of eighty-eight, Thay continued to have extraordinary new insights into fundamental Buddhist teachings. Sometimes, with great delight, he would return from a walking meditation, pick up his brush, and capture these insights in short calligraphy phrases—many of which are included in these pages.

This remarkable book, edited by his monastic students, captures the essence of the last two years of Thay's lectures on the art of mindful living. In particular, it presents his groundbreaking teach-ings from a twenty-one-day retreat in June 2014, at Plum Village Mindfulness Practice Center in France, on the theme: "What Hap-pens When We Die? What Happens When We Are Alive?"

I never cease to be deeply moved by the ways in which Thay truly embodies his teachings. He is a master of the art of living.

He cherishes life and, despite all the adverse conditions he has encountered over the years—including war, exile, betrayal, and ill health—he has never given up. He has taken refuge in his breathing and in the wonders of the present moment. Thay is a survivor. He has survived thanks to the love of his students and his community, and thanks to the nourishment he receives from his meditation, mindful breathing, and relaxing moments walking and resting in nature. In times of war and hardship, as well as in times of peace and harmony, I have seen how the wisdom you find in these pages has enabled Thay to embrace life's joys and pains with fearlessness, compassion, faith, and hope. I wish you all every success in applying the teachings in this book in your own life, following in his footsteps, so you may bring healing, love, and happiness to yourselves, your family, and the world.

Sister Chan Khong

INTRODUCTION

———

We're so close to Earth that sometimes we forget how beautiful it is. Seen from space, our blue planet is remarkably alive—a living paradise suspended in a vast and hostile cosmos. On the first trip to the moon, astronauts were stunned to see Earth rise above the moon's desolate horizon. We know that on the moon there are no trees, rivers, or birds. No other planet has yet been found to have life as we know it. It is reported that astronauts orbiting high up in space stations spend most of their free time contemplating the breathtaking sight of Earth far below. From a distance, it looks like one giant living, breathing organism. Seeing its beauty and wonder, astronauts feel great love for the whole Earth. They know billions of people are living out their lives on this little planet, with all their joy, happiness, and suffering. They see violence, wars, famine, and environmental destruction. At the same time, they see clearly that this wonderful little blue planet, so fragile and precious, is irreplaceable. As one astronaut put it, "We went to the moon as technicians; we returned as humanitarians."

Science is the pursuit of understanding, helping us to understand distant stars and galaxies, our place in the cosmos, as well as the intimate fabric of matter, living cells, and our own bodies. Science, like philosophy, is concerned with understanding the nature of existence and the meaning of life.

Spirituality is also a field of research and study. We want to understand ourselves, the world around us, and what it means to be alive on Earth. We want to discover who we really are, and we want to understand our suffering. Understanding our suffering gives rise to acceptance and love, and this is what determines our quality of life. We all need to be understood and to be loved. And we all want to understand and to love.

Spirituality is not religion. It is a path for us to generate happiness, understanding, and love, so we can live deeply each moment of our life. Having a spiritual dimension in our lives does not mean escaping life or dwelling in a place of bliss outside this world but discovering ways to handle life's difficulties and generate peace, joy, and happiness right where we are, on this beautiful planet.

The spirit of practicing mindfulness, concentration, and insight in Buddhism is very close to the spirit of science. We don't use expensive instruments but rather our clear mind and our stillness to look deeply and investigate reality for ourselves, with openness and non-discrimination. We want to know where we come from and where we are going. And most of all, we want to be happy. Humanity has given rise to many talented artists, musicians, and architects, but how many of us have mastered the art of creating a happy moment—for ourselves and those around us?

Like every species on Earth, we are always seeking the ideal conditions that will allow us to live to our fullest potential. We want to do more than just survive. We want to live. But what does it mean to be alive? What does it mean to die? What happens when we die? Is there life after death? Is there reincarnation? Will we see our loved ones again? Do we have a soul that goes to heaven or nirvana or God? These questions are in everyone's hearts. Sometimes they become words, and sometimes they are left unsaid, but they are still there, pulling at our hearts every time we think about our life, about those we love, our sick or ageing parents, or those who have already passed away.

How can we begin to answer these questions about life and death? A good answer, the right answer, should be based on evidence. It is not a question of faith or belief, but of looking deeply. To meditate is to look deeply and see the things that others cannot see, including the wrong views that lie at the base of our suffering. When we can break free from these wrong views, we can master the art of living happily in peace and freedom.

The first wrong view we need to liberate ourselves from is the idea that we are a separate self cut off from the rest of the world. We have a tendency to think we have a separate self that is born at one moment and must die at another, and that is permanent during the time we are alive. As long as we have this wrong view, we will suffer; we will create suffering for those around us, and we will cause harm to other species and to our precious planet. The second wrong view that many of us hold is the view that we are only this body, and that when we die we cease to exist. This wrong view blinds us to all the ways in which we are interconnected with the world around us and the ways in which we continue after death. The third wrong view that many of us have is the idea that what we are looking for—whether it be happiness, heaven, or love—can be found only outside us in a distant future. We may spend our lives chasing after and waiting for these things, not realizing that they can be found within us, right in the present moment.

There are three fundamental practices to help liberate us from these three wrong views: the concentrations on *emptiness, signlessness,* and *aimlessness.* They are known as the Three Doors of Liberation and are available in every school of Buddhism. These three concentrations offer us a deep insight into what it means to be alive and what it means to die. They help us transform feelings of grief, anxiety, loneliness, and alienation. They have the power to liberate us from our wrong views, so we can live deeply and fully, and face dying and death without fear, anger, or despair.

We can also explore four additional concentrations on *impermanence, non-craving, letting go,* and *nirvana.* These four practices are found in *Sutra on the Full Awareness of Breathing,* a wonderful text from early Buddhism. The concentration on *impermanence* helps free us from our tendency to live as though we and our loved ones will be here forever. The concentration on *non-craving* is an opportunity to take time to sit down and figure out what true happiness really is. We discover that we already have more than enough conditions to be happy, right here in the present moment. And the concentration on *letting go* helps us disentangle ourselves from suffering and transform and release painful feelings. Looking deeply with all these concentrations, we are able to touch the peace and freedom of *nirvana.*

These seven concentrations are very practical. Together, they awaken us to reality. They help us cherish what we have, so we can touch true happiness in the very here and now. And they give us the insight we need to treasure the time we have, reconcile with those we love, and transform our suffering into love and understanding. This is the art of living.

We need to use our mindfulness, concentration, and insight in order to understand what it means to be alive and what it means to die. We can speak of scientific and spiritual discoveries as "insights" and the practice of nourishing and sustaining those insights as "concentration."

With the insights of science and spirituality, we have an opportunity in the twenty-first century to conquer the root causes of suffering in human beings. If the twentieth century was characterized by individualism and consumption, the twenty-first century can be characterized by the insight of interconnectedness, and by efforts to explore new forms of solidarity and togetherness. Meditating on the seven concentrations enables us to see everything in the light of interdependence, freeing us from our wrong views and breaking down the barriers of a discriminating mind. The freedom we seek is not the kind of freedom that is self-destructive or destructive of other nations or the environment, but the kind of freedom that liberates us from our loneliness, anger, hatred, fear, craving, and despair.

The teaching of the Buddha is very clear, effective, and simple to understand. It opens up a path of living, not just for our personal benefit, but for our whole species. We have the power to decide the destiny of our planet. Buddhism offers us the clearest expression of humanism we have ever had. It is our insights and our actions that will save us. If we awaken to our true situation, there will be collective change in our consciousness. Then hope will be possible.

Let us explore how the seven concentrations—deep insights into reality—can shine light on our situation, our suffering. If while reading you find yourself in unfamiliar terrain, just breathe. This book is a journey we make together, like taking a walk through the forest, enjoying the breathtaking wonders of our precious planet. Occasionally there is a tree with beautiful bark, a striking rock formation, or some vibrant moss growing just off the path, and we want our companion to also enjoy the same beauty. Sometime along the path we'll sit and have lunch together, or further on the journey drink from a clear spring. This book is a bit like that. Occasionally we will stop and rest, to have a little drink, or to simply sit there, the stillness between us already complete.

STILLNESS

In Plum Village, the mindfulness practice center in France where I live, there used to be a veranda called the Listening to the Rain Veranda. We made it specially for that purpose—so we could sit there and listen to the rain and not need to think about anything. Listening to the rain can help the mind come to stillness.

Bringing the mind to stillness is easy. You need only to pay attention to one thing. As long as your mind is listening to the rain it is not thinking about anything else. You don't need to try to still your mind. You need only to relax and continue listening to the rain. The longer you are able to do so, the more still your mind becomes.

Sitting in stillness like this allows us to see things as they truly are. When the body is relaxed and the mind comes to rest, we can see clearly. We become as still and clear as the water in a mountain lake whose tranquil surface reflects the blue sky above, the clouds, and the surrounding rocky peaks just as they are.

As long as we're restless and the mind is unsettled, we won't be able to see reality clearly. We'll be like the lake on a windy day, its surface troubled, reflecting a distorted view of the sky. But as soon as we restore our stillness, we can look deeply and begin to see the truth.

PRACTICE: THE ART OF BREATHING

Mindful breathing is a wonderful way to calm the body and your feelings, and to restore stillness and peace. It's not difficult to breathe mindfully. Anyone can do it—even children.

When you breathe mindfully, you bring your whole body and mind into harmony, concentrating on the wonder of the breath. Our breathing is as beautiful as music.

Breathing in, you know you are breathing in. You bring all your attention to your in-breath. As you breathe in, there is peace and harmony in the whole body.

As you breathe out, you *know* you are breathing out. As you breathe out, there is calming, relaxation, and letting go. You allow all the muscles in your face and shoulders to relax.

You don't have to force yourself to breathe in and out. You don't have to make any effort at all. You don't have to interfere with your breathing. Just allow it to take place naturally.

As you breathe in and out, imagine someone playing a very long note on a violin, drawing the bow back and forth across the string. The note sounds continuous. If you were to draw an image of your breath, it would look like a figure eight, not a straight line, because there is continuity as your breath flows in and out. Your breathing becomes the music itself.

Breathing like this is mindfulness, and as you sustain mindfulness, that is concentration. Wherever there is concentration, there is insight—a breakthrough—bringing more peace, understanding, love, and joy into your life.

Before we continue, let us enjoy a few moments to listen to the music of our breathing together.

Breathing in, I enjoy my in-breath.
Breathing out, I enjoy my out-breath.

Breathing in, my whole body is harmonized with the in-breath.
Breathing out, my whole body is calmed with the out-breath.

Breathing in, my whole body enjoys the peace of my in-breath.
Breathing out, my whole body enjoys the relaxation of my out-breath.

Breathing in, I enjoy the harmony of my in-breath.
Breathing out, I enjoy the harmony of my out-breath.

CHAPTER 1

EMPTINESS
THE WONDER OF INTERBEING

Emptiness means to be full of everything
but empty of a separate existence.

Imagine, for a moment, a beautiful flower. That flower might be an orchid or a rose, or even a simple little daisy growing beside a path. Looking into a flower, we can see that it is full of life. It contains soil, rain, and sunshine. It is also full of clouds, oceans, and minerals. It is even full of space and time. In fact, the whole cosmos is present in this one little flower. If we took out just one of these "non-flower" elements, the flower would not be there. Without the soil's nutrients, the flower could not grow. Without rain and sunshine, the flower would die. And if we removed all the non-flower elements, there would be nothing substantive left that we could call a "flower." So our observation tells us that the flower is full of the whole cosmos, while at the same time it is empty of a separate self-existence. The flower cannot exist by itself alone.

We too are full of so many things and yet empty of a separate self. Like the flower, we contain earth, water, air, sunlight, and warmth. We contain space and consciousness. We contain our ancestors, our parents and grandparents, education, food, and culture. The whole cosmos has come together to create the wonderful manifestation that we are. If we remove any of these "non-us" elements, we will find there is no "us" left.

EMPTINESS: THE FIRST DOOR OF LIBERATION

Emptiness does not mean nothingness. Saying that we are empty does not mean that we do not exist. No matter if something is full or empty, that thing clearly needs to be there in the first place. When we say a cup is empty, the cup must be there in order to be empty. When we say that we are empty, it means that we must be there in order to be empty of a permanent, separate self.

About thirty years ago I was looking for an English word to describe our deep interconnection with everything else. I liked the word "togetherness," but I finally came up with the word "interbeing." The verb "to be" can be misleading, because we cannot be by ourselves, alone. "To be" is always to "inter-be." If we combine the prefix "inter" with the verb "to be," we have a new verb, "inter-be." To inter-be reflects reality more accurately. We inter-are with one another and with all life.

There is a biologist named Lewis Thomas, whose work I appreciate very much. He describes how our human bodies are "shared, rented, and occupied" by countless other tiny organisms, without whom we couldn't "move a muscle, drum a finger, or think a thought." Our body is a community, and the trillions of non-human cells in our body are even more numerous than the human cells. Without them, we could not be here in this moment. Without them, we wouldn't be able to think, to feel, or to speak. There are, he says, no solitary beings. The whole planet is one giant, living, breathing cell, with all its working parts linked in symbiosis.

THE INSIGHT OF INTERBEING

We can observe emptiness and interbeing everywhere in our daily life. If we look at a child, it's easy to see the child's mother and father, grandmother and grandfather, in her. The way she looks, the way she acts, the things she says. Even her skills and talents are the same as her parents'. If at times we cannot understand why the child is acting a certain way, it is helpful to remember that she is not a separate self-entity. She is a *continuation*. Her parents and ancestors are inside her. When she walks and talks, they walk and talk as well. Looking into the child, we can be in touch with her parents and ancestors, but equally, looking into the parent, we can see the child. We do not exist independently. We inter-are. Everything relies on everything else in the cosmos in order to manifest—whether a star, a cloud, a flower, a tree, or you and me.

I remember one time when I was in London, doing walking meditation along the street, and I saw a book displayed in a bookshop window with the title *My Mother, Myself*. I didn't buy the book because I felt I already knew what was inside. It's true that each one of us is a continuation of our mother; we *are* our mother. And so whenever we are angry at our mother or father, we are also being angry at ourselves. Whatever we do, our parents are doing it with us. This may be hard to accept, but it's the truth. We can't say we don't want to have anything to do with our parents. They are in us, and we are in them. We are the continuation of all our ancestors. Thanks to impermanence, we have a chance to transform our inheritance in a beautiful direction.

Every time I offer incense or prostrate before the altar in my hermitage, I do not do this as an individual self but as a whole lineage. Whenever I walk, sit, eat, or practice calligraphy, I do so with the awareness that all my ancestors are within me in that moment. I am their continuation. Whatever I am doing, the energy of mindfulness enables me to do it as "us," not as "me." When I hold a calligraphy brush, I know I cannot remove my father from my hand. I know I cannot remove my mother or my ancestors from me. They are present in all my cells, in my gestures, in my capacity to draw a beautiful circle. Nor can I remove my spiritual teachers from my hand. They are there in the peace, concentration, and mindfulness I enjoy as I make the circle. We are all drawing the circle together. There is no separate self doing it. While practicing calligraphy, I touch the profound insight of no self. It becomes a deep practice of meditation.

Whether we're at work or at home, we can practice to see all our ancestors and teachers present in our actions. We can see their presence when we express a talent or skill they have transmitted to us. We can see their hands in ours as we prepare a meal or wash the dishes. We can experience profound connection and free ourselves from the idea that we are a separate self.

YOU ARE A RIVER

We can contemplate emptiness in terms of interbeing across space—our relationship to everything and everyone around us. We can also contemplate emptiness in terms of impermanence across time. Impermanence means that nothing remains the same thing in two consecutive moments. The Greek philosopher Heraclitus of Ephesus said, "You can never bathe in the same river twice." The river is always flowing, so as soon as we climb out onto the bank and then return again to bathe, the water has already changed. And even in that short space of time we too have changed. In our body, cells are dying and being born every second. Our thoughts, perceptions, feelings, and state of mind are also changing from one moment to the next. So we cannot swim twice in the same river; nor can the river receive the same person twice. Our body and mind are an ever-changing continuum. Although we seem to look the same, and we are still called the same name, we are different. No matter how sophisticated our scientific instruments, we cannot find anything in our person that remains the same and that we can call a soul or a self. Once we accept the reality of impermanence, we have to also accept the truth of no self.

The two concentrations on emptiness and impermanence help free us from our tendency to think that we are separate selves. They are insights that can help us step out of the prison of our wrong views. We have to train ourselves to sustain the insight of emptiness while we're looking at a person, a bird, a tree, or a rock. It's very different from just sitting there and speculating about emptiness. We have to really *see* the nature of emptiness, of interbeing, of impermanence, in ourselves and others.

For example, you call me Vietnamese. You may be quite sure that I'm a Vietnamese monk. But in fact, legally speaking, I don't have a Vietnamese passport. Culturally speaking, I have elements of French in me, as well as Chinese culture and even Indian culture. In my writing and teachings, you can discover several sources of cultural streams. And ethnically speaking, there's no such race as the Vietnamese race. In me there are Melanesian elements, Indonesian elements, and Mongolian elements. Just as the flower is made of non-flower elements, so am I made of non-me elements. The insight of interbeing helps us touch this wisdom of non-discrimination. It sets us free. We no longer want to belong just to one geographical area or cultural identity. We see the presence of the whole cosmos in us. The more we look with the insight of emptiness, the more we discover and the deeper we understand. This naturally brings compassion, freedom, and non-fear.

PLEASE CALL ME BY MY TRUE NAMES

I remember one day in the 1970s, while we were working for the Vietnamese Buddhist Peace Delegation in Paris, some terrible news came in. Many people had been fleeing Vietnam by boat, which was always a very dangerous journey. Not only was there the danger of storms and not having enough fuel, food, or water, but also there was the risk of getting attacked by pirates, who were active along the coast of Thailand. The story we heard was tragic. Pirates had boarded a boat, stolen valuables, and raped an eleven-year-old girl. When her father tried to intervene, he was thrown overboard. After the attack, the girl threw herself overboard too. Both perished in the sea.

After I heard this news, I couldn't sleep. The feelings of sadness, compassion, and pity were very strong. But as a practitioner, we cannot let the feelings of anger and helplessness paralyze us. So I practiced walking meditation, sitting meditation, and mindful breathing to look more deeply into the situation, to try to understand.

I visualized myself as a little boy born into a poor family in Thailand, my father an illiterate fisherman. From one generation to the next, my ancestors had lived in poverty, without education, without help. I too grew up without an education, and perhaps with violence. Then one day, someone asks me to go out to sea and make a fortune as a pirate and I foolishly agree, desperate to finally break out of this terrible cycle of poverty. And then, under pressure from my fellow pirates, and with no coastal patrol to stop me, I force myself on a beautiful young girl.

My whole life I have never been taught how to love or understand. I never received an education. Nobody showed me a future. If you had been there on the boat with a gun, you could have shot me. You could have killed me. But you wouldn't have been able to help me.

Meditating that night in Paris, I saw that hundreds of babies continue to be born under similar circumstances and that they will grow up to be pirates, unless I do something now to help them. I saw all of this, and my anger disappeared. My heart was full of the energy of compassion and forgiveness. I could embrace not only the eleven-year-old girl in my arms, but also the pirate. I could see myself in them. This is the fruit of the contemplation on emptiness, on interbeing. I could see that suffering is not only individual; it is also collective. Suffering can be transmitted to us by our ancestors, or it can be there in the society around us. As my blame and hatred dissipated, I became determined to live my life in such a way that I could help not only the victims, but also the perpetrators.

So, if you call me Thich Nhat Hanh, I will say, "Yes, that is me." And if you call me the young girl, I will say, "Yes, that is me." If you call me the pirate, I will also say, "Yes, that is me." These are all my true names. If you call me an impoverished child in a war zone with no future, I will say, "Yes, that is me." And if you call me the arms merchant selling weapons to support that war, I will say, "Yes, that is me." All of these people are us. We inter-are with everyone.

When we can free ourselves from the idea of separateness,
we have compassion, we have understanding,
and we have the energy we need to help.

TWO LEVELS OF TRUTH

In everyday language, we say "you" and "I" and "we" and "they" because these designations are useful. They identify who or what we are talking about, but it is important to realize they are only conventional designations. They are only relative truths, not the ultimate truth. We are so much more than these labels and categories. It is impossible to draw a hard line between you and I and the rest of the cosmos. The insight of interbeing helps us connect with the ultimate truth of emptiness. The teaching on emptiness is not about the "dying" of the self. The self does not need to die. The self is just an idea, an illusion, a wrong view, a notion; it is not reality. How can something that is not there die? We do not need to kill the self, but we can remove the illusion of a separate self by gaining a deeper understanding of reality.

NO OWNER, NO BOSS

When we think of ourselves as having a separate self, a separate existence, we identify with our thoughts and our body. We have the impression that we are the boss or owner of our body. We might think "This is my body" or "This is my mind" in the same way we might think "This is my house," "This is my car," "These are my qualifications," "These are my feelings," "These are my emotions," "This is my suffering." In fact, we should not be so sure.

When we think or work or breathe, many of us believe there must be a person, an actor, behind our actions. We believe there must be "someone" doing the action. But when the wind blows, there is no blower behind the wind. There is only the wind, and if it does not blow, it is not the wind at all. When we say "It is raining," there does not need to be a rainer in order to have the rain. Who is the "it" that is raining? There is only raining. Raining is happening.

In the same way, outside of our actions, there is no person, no thing we can call our "self." When we think, we are our thinking. When we work, we are the working. When we breathe, we are the breathing. When we act, we are our actions.

I remember once seeing a cartoon depicting the French philosopher René Descartes standing in front of a horse. Descartes was pointing his finger up in the air, declaring, "I think, therefore I am." Behind him the horse was wondering, "Therefore you are *what?*"

Descartes was trying to demonstrate that a self exists. Because, according to his logic, if I am thinking, then there must be a "me" that exists in order to do the thinking. If I am not there, then who is thinking?

We cannot deny that there is thinking. It is clear that thinking is taking place. Most of the time the problem is that too much thinking is taking place—thinking about yesterday, worrying about tomorrow—and all of this thinking takes us away from ourselves and from the here and now. When we are caught up in thinking about the past and the future, our mind is not with our body; it is not in contact with the life within us and around us in the present moment. So it might be more accurate to say:

I think (too much),
therefore I am (not there to live my life).

The most accurate way to describe the process of thinking is not that there is "someone" thinking but that *thinking is manifesting,* as the result of a remarkable, wondrous coming together of conditions. We do not need to have a self in order to think; there is thinking and only thinking. There is not an additional separate entity doing the thinking. Insofar as there is a thinker, the thinker comes into existence at the same time as the thinking. It is like the left and the right. You cannot have the one without the other, but you also cannot have the one before the other; they manifest at the same time. As soon as there is a left, there is also a right. As soon as there's a thought, there's a thinker. The thinker *is* the thinking.

The same is true with the body and action. Millions of neurons work together in our brain, in constant communication. They act in concert, producing a movement, a feeling, a thought, or a perception. Yet there is no conductor of the orchestra. There is no boss making all the decisions. We cannot locate a place in the brain or anywhere else in the body that is controlling everything. There are the actions of thinking, feeling, and perceiving, but there is no actor or separate self-entity doing the thinking, feeling, and perceiving.

In 1966, in London, I had a very powerful experience contemplating a corpse in the British Museum. It had been naturally preserved in sand, lying in the fetal position, for more than five thousand years. I stood there for a long time, very concentrated, contemplating the body.

A few weeks later, in Paris, I woke up suddenly in the middle of the night and wanted to touch my legs to check that I had not become a corpse like that. It was two o'clock, and I sat up. I contemplated the corpse and my own body. After sitting for about an hour, I felt like water raining down on a mountain—washing, washing. Finally, I got up and wrote a poem. I called it "The Great Lion's Roar." The feeling was so clear and the images flowed freely; they gushed out, like a huge water container being overturned. The poem opened with these lines:

> *A white cloud floats in the sky*
> *A bouquet of flowers blooms*
> *Floating clouds*
> *Blooming flowers*
> *The clouds are the floating*
> *The flowers are the blooming*

I saw very clearly that if a cloud is not floating, it is not a cloud. If a flower is not blooming, it is not a flower. Without floating, there is no cloud. Without blooming, there is no flower. We cannot separate the two. You cannot take the mind out of the body, and you cannot take the body out of the mind. They inter-are. Just as we find the flower in the blooming, we find a human being in the energy of action. If there's no energy of action, there's no human being. As the French existentialist philosopher Jean-Paul Sartre famously said, "Man is the sum of his actions." We are the sum of everything we think, say, and do. Just as an orange tree produces beautiful blossoms, leaves, and fruit, so do we produce thinking, speech, and action. And just like the orange tree, our actions are always ripening over time. We can find ourselves only in our actions of body, speech, and mind, continuing as energy across space and time.

NOT IN A STUPA

Over ten years ago, one of my disciples in Vietnam had a stupa—a Buddhist shrine—built for my ashes. I told her that I didn't need a stupa for my ashes. I don't want to be stuck in a stupa. I want to be everywhere.

"But," she protested, "it's already built!"

"In that case," I said, "you'll have to put an inscription on the front, saying, 'I am not in here.'" It's true. I won't be there in the stupa. Even if my body is cremated and the ashes are put in there, they aren't me. I won't be in there. Why would I want to be in there when outside it is so beautiful?

But in case some people misunderstand, I told her they might need to add another inscription, saying, "I am not out there either." People won't find me inside or outside the stupa. Yet they may still misunderstand. So there may need to be a third inscription that reads, "If I am to be found anywhere, it is in your peaceful way of breathing and walking." That is my continuation. Even though we may never have met in person, if, when you breathe in, you find peace in your breathing, I am there with you.

I often tell a story from the Bible, from the book of Luke, about two disciples traveling to Emmaus after Jesus had died. They met a man along the road and began to talk and walk with him. After some time, they stopped at an inn to eat. When the two disciples observed the way the man broke the bread and poured the wine, they recognized Jesus.

This story teaches that even Jesus is not to be found only in his physical body. His living reality extends far beyond his physical body. Jesus was fully present in the way the bread was broken and in the way the wine was poured. That is the living Christ. That is why he can say, "Where two or three gather in my name, there am I among them." It is not only Jesus or the Buddha or any other great spiritual teacher who is with us after their death; all of us continue as energy long after our physical body has changed form.

YOUR BELOVED IS NOT A SELF

When we prostrate before the Buddha or we bow to Jesus Christ, are we bowing to the Buddha who lived 2,500 years ago or to the Christ who lived 2,000 years ago? Who are we bowing to? Are we bowing to a self? We have learned that the Buddha and Jesus Christ were human beings like us. All human beings are made of the five ever-changing, ever-flowing rivers of the physical body, feelings, perceptions, mental formations, and consciousness. You, me, Jesus Christ, and the Buddha—we are all continually changing.

To say that today Jesus Christ is exactly the same as he was 2,000 years ago is a mistake, because even in the thirty years of his life, Jesus Christ was never exactly the same. He changed every month and every year, and the same is true for the Buddha. At the age of thirty, the Buddha was different from how he was at the age of forty. And at the age of eighty, he was different again. He, like all of us, constantly evolved and changed. So which Buddha do we want? The one at eighty years old or at forty? We may visualize the Buddha with a certain kind of face or a certain kind of body, but we know that his body is impermanent and ever changing. Or we might think that the Buddha doesn't exist anymore or that the Jesus Christ of the past is no longer here. But that would also be incorrect, because we know that nothing can be lost.

The Buddha is not a separate self; he is his actions. What are his actions? His actions are the practice of freedom and awakening in the service of all beings, and these actions continue. The Buddha is still here, but not in the form we usually imagine.

Each one of us can be in direct contact with the Buddha as a kind of action. When we are able to walk happily on the Earth, in touch with the wonders of life—with the beautiful birds, trees, and blue sky—feeling happy, at peace, and at ease, then we ourselves are a continuation of the Buddha. The Buddha is not something outside us. He is a kind of energy within us. Every day the living buddha is evolving and growing, manifesting in new forms.

HOW OLD WILL YOU BE IN HEAVEN?

In our Buddhist Peace Delegation office in Paris in the 1970s there was an English woman who volunteered to help us in our work. Although she was over seventy years old, she was in very good health, and every morning she would climb up the five flights of stairs to our office. She was Anglican and had a very strong faith. She firmly believed that after she died she would go to heaven, where she would be reunited with her very kind and handsome husband, who had died when he was thirty-three.

One day I asked her, "After you die and go to heaven and meet your husband again, will he be thirty-three or seventy or eighty? And how old will you be? It would be strange for you, over seventy, to meet him at thirty-three." Sometimes our faith is very simple.

She was confused, because she had never asked herself that question. She had just assumed that they would meet again. With the insight of interbeing—the insight that we inter-are with one another and with all life—we don't need to wait to meet our beloved ones again in heaven. They are still right here with us.

NOTHING IS LOST

There are those who believe that an eternal self continues to exist after the body disintegrates. We could call this belief a kind of "eternalism." Others believe that after death there is nothing. This is a kind of "nihilism." We need to avoid both these extremes. The insight of impermanence and interbeing tells us there cannot be an eternal, separate self, and the first law of thermodynamics—the law of conservation of energy—tells us that nothing can be created or destroyed; it can only be transformed. So it's not scientific to believe that after our body decomposes we become nothing.

While we are alive, our life is energy, and after death, we continue to be energy. That energy is continually changing and transforming. It can never be lost.

We cannot assert that after death there is nothing.
Something can never become nothing.

If we have lost someone who is very close to us and we are grieving, the concentrations on emptiness and signlessness help us look deeply and see the ways in which they still continue. Our loved one is still alive within us and around us. They are very real. We have not lost them. It is possible to still recognize them in a different form or in even more beautiful forms than in the past.

In the light of emptiness and interbeing we know they have not died or disappeared: they continue in their actions and in us. We can still talk to them. We can say something like, "I know you are there. I'm breathing for you. I'm smiling for you. I'm enjoying looking around with your eyes. I am enjoying life with you. I know that you are still there very close to me, and that now you continue in me."

LIFE FORCE

If there is no boss, no owner, no actor, behind our actions and no thinker behind our thoughts, then why do we have this sense of self? In Buddhist psychology, the part of our consciousness that has a tendency to create a sense of self is known in Sanskrit as *manas*. Manas is equivalent to what Sigmund Freud in psychoanalysis called the "id." Manas manifests from deep in our consciousness. It is our survival instinct, and it always urges us to avoid pain and seek pleasure. Manas keeps saying, "This is me; this is my body; this is mine," because manas is unable to perceive reality clearly. Manas tries to protect and defend what it mistakenly thinks is a self. But this is not always good for our survival. Manas cannot see that we are made of only non-us elements and that what it considers to be a self is not actually a separate entity. Manas cannot see that its wrong view of a self can bring us a lot of suffering and prevent us from living happily with freedom. Contemplating the interconnectedness between our body and our environment, we can help manas transform its delusion and see the truth.

We don't need to get rid of manas; manas is a natural part of life. The reason manas calls this body "me" and "mine" is because one of manas's roles is to maintain our life force. This life force is what the twentieth-century French philosopher Henri Bergson called *élan vital*. Like all species, we have a will to live and a strong desire to cling to and protect our life and to defend ourselves from danger. But we have to be cautious not to let our instinct of self-preservation and auto-defense mislead us into thinking we have a separate self. The insight of interbeing and no self can help us make use of our life force—what Freud called sublimation—to take action in life to help and protect others, to forgive and to reconcile, and to help and protect the Earth.

I remember I once left a piece of ginger in a corner in my hermitage and didn't tend to it. But then one day I discovered that it had sprouted. The stem of ginger was giving rise to a plant of ginger. There was life within it. The same thing can happen with a potato. Everything has this vitality of wanting to go forward and be continued. This is very natural. Everything wants to live. So I put the ginger in a pot with some earth and let it grow.

When a woman becomes pregnant, there is already a life force driving that child's development. The life force of the mother and of the fetus are neither the same nor different. The life force of the mother enters the child and the life force of the child enters the mother. They are one, and little by little they separate from each other. But sometimes we think that when the baby is born, it is as if the child now has a separate self, as its body, feelings, perceptions, mental formations, and consciousness are different from those of the mother. We may think that we can separate the child from the mother, but the truth is that there remains a relationship of continuation. Looking at the child we see the mother, and looking at the mother we see the child.

PRACTICE: YOUR MOTHER'S HAND

Remember the times you were sick with a fever when you were a little boy or girl? Remember how awful it felt to be so sick? But then your mother or father, or perhaps a grandparent, would put their hand on your burning forehead and it felt so wonderful. You could feel the nectar of love in their hand, and that was enough to comfort and reassure you. Just knowing they were there, beside you, brought relief. If you do not live close to your mother anymore, or if your mother is no longer present in her usual bodily form, you have to look deeply to see that she is in fact always with you. You carry your mother in every cell of your body. Her hand is still in your hand. If your parents have already passed away and you practice looking deeply like this, you can have an even closer relationship with your parents than that of someone whose parents are still alive but who cannot communicate easily with them.

You may like to take a moment now to look at your hand. Can you see your mother's hand in your hand? Or your father's? Look deeply into your hand. With this insight, and with all the love and care of your parents, bring your hand up to your forehead and feel the hand of your mother or father touching your forehead. Allow yourself to be cared for by your parents in you. They are always with you.

LIVING BEINGS

We have a tendency to distinguish between animate and inanimate life-forms. But observation shows there is life force even in the objects we call inanimate. Life force and consciousness are in a stem of ginger or in an acorn. The ginger knows how to become a plant, and the acorn knows how to become an oak tree. We cannot call these things inanimate, because they know what to do. Even a subatomic particle or a speck of dust has vitality. There is no absolute dividing line between animate and inanimate, between living matter and inert matter. In so-called inert matter there is life, and living beings are dependent on so-called inert matter. If we took the so-called inanimate elements out of you and me, we would not be able to live. We are made of non-human elements. This is what is taught in the Diamond Sutra, an ancient Buddhist text that could be considered the world's first treatise on deep ecology. We cannot draw a hard distinction between human beings and other living beings, or between living beings and inert matter.

There is vitality in everything.
The entire cosmos is radiant with vitality.

If we see the Earth as just a block of matter lying outside of us, then we have not yet truly seen the Earth. We need to be able to see that we are a part of the Earth, and to see that the entire Earth is in us. The Earth is also alive; it has intelligence and creativity. If the Earth were inert matter, it could not give birth to countless great beings, including the Buddha, Jesus Christ, Muhammad, and Moses. The Earth is also mother to our parents and to us. Looking with the eyes of non-discrimination, we can establish a very close relationship with the Earth. We look at the Earth with our heart and not the eyes of cold reasoning. You are the planet, and the planet is you. The well-being of your body is not possible without the well-being of the planet. And that is why to protect the well-being of your body we must protect the well-being of the planet. This is the insight of emptiness.

ARE YOU A SOULMATE OF THE BUDDHA?

At the time of the Buddha, there were countless religious and spiritual teachers, each advocating a different spiritual path and practice, and each claiming their teachings were the best and the most correct. One day a group of young people came to ask the Buddha, "Of all these teachers, whom should we believe?"

"Don't believe anything, not even what I tell you!" replied the Buddha. "Even if it's an ancient teaching, even if it's taught by a highly revered teacher. You should use your intelligence and critical mind to carefully examine everything you see or hear. And then put the teaching into practice to see if it helps liberate you from your suffering and your difficulties. If it does, you can believe in it." If we want to be a soulmate of the Buddha, we need to have a discriminating, critical mind like this.

If we do not allow our beliefs to evolve, if we do not maintain an open mind, we risk waking up one day to discover that we have lost faith in what we once believed. This can be devastating. As practitioners of meditation, we should never accept anything on blind faith, regarding it as absolute, unchanging truth. We should investigate and observe reality with mindfulness and concentration, so our understanding and faith can deepen day by day. This is the kind of faith we cannot lose, because it is not based on ideas or beliefs but on experienced reality.

IS THERE REINCARNATION?

Many of us are resistant to the idea that one day we will die. At the same time, we want to know what happens when we die. Some of us believe we will go to heaven and live happily there. For others, it seems life is too short and we want another chance, to do better next time around. This is why the idea of reincarnation seems very appealing. We may hope that the people who have committed acts of violence will be brought to justice in the next life and be made to pay for their crimes. Or perhaps we're afraid of nothingness, of oblivion, of not existing anymore. And so, when our body starts to age and disintegrate, it's tempting to think we might have the opportunity to start again in a young and healthy body, like discarding worn-out clothes.

The idea of reincarnation suggests there is a separate soul, self, or spirit that somehow leaves the body at death, flies away, and then reincarnates in another body. It's as though the body is some kind of house for the mind, soul, or spirit. This implies that the mind and body can be separated from each other, and that although the body is impermanent, the mind and spirit are somehow permanent. But neither of these ideas is in accord with the deepest teachings of Buddhism.

We can speak of two kinds of Buddhism: popular Buddhism and deep Buddhism. Different audiences need different kinds of teachings, so the teachings should always be adapted in order to be appropriate to the audience. This is why there are thousands of different points of entry into the teachings, enabling many kinds of people to benefit and experience transformation and relief from their suffering. In popular Buddhist culture, it is said there are countless hell realms that we can fall into after dying. Many temples display vivid illustrations of what can happen to us in the hell realms—for example, if we lie in this lifetime, our tongue will be cut out in the next. This is a kind of "skillful means" to motivate people to live their lives in more ethical ways. This approach may help some people, but it may not help others.

Although these teachings are *not* in accord with the ultimate truth, many people benefit from them. Nevertheless, with compassion, skill, and understanding, we may be able to help one another gradually release our current views and deepen our understanding. If we want to open up to a new way of looking at life and death and what happens after death, we need to let go of our present views in order to allow a deeper understanding to emerge. If we want to climb a ladder, we have to let go of one rung in order to reach the next one. If we cling to the views we presently hold, we cannot progress.

In the beginning, I had certain ideas about mindfulness, meditation, and Buddhism. After ten years of practice, I had a much better understanding. Then after forty or fifty years, my insight and understanding had become even deeper. We are all on a path, we are all making progress, and along the way we need to be ready to abandon our current view so we can be open to a new, better, and deeper view, one which brings us closer to the truth; one which is more helpful for transforming our suffering and cultivating happiness. Whatever views we hold, we should be careful not to get caught up in thinking that our view is the "best" and that only *we* have the truth. The spirit of Buddhism is very tolerant. We should always keep our hearts open to the people who have different views or beliefs. Practicing openness and non-attachment to views is fundamental in Buddhism. That is why, even though there are dozens of different schools of Buddhism, Buddhists have never waged a holy war against each other.

THE CREAM OF THE BUDDHA'S TEACHING

The spiritual context of ancient India had a strong influence on the Buddha's teachings. Buddhism is made of non-Buddhist elements in the same way that a flower is made of non-flower elements. In the West, Buddhism is often associated with the ideas of reincarnation, karma, and retribution, but these are not originally Buddhist concepts. They were already well established when the Buddha began teaching. In fact, they were not at all at the heart of what the Buddha taught.

In ancient India, reincarnation, karma, and retribution were all taught based on the idea of the existence of a self. There was a widely held belief in a permanent self that reincarnated and received karmic retribution for actions in this lifetime. But when the Buddha taught reincarnation, karma, and retribution, he taught them in the light of no self, impermanence, and nirvana—our true nature of no birth and no death. He taught that it is not necessary to have a separate, unchanging self in order for karma—actions of body, speech, and mind—to be continued.

According to the Buddha's core teachings on no self, impermanence, and interbeing, the mind is not a separate entity. The mind cannot leave the body and reincarnate somewhere else. If the mind or spirit is taken from the body, the spirit no longer exists. Body and mind depend on each other in order to exist. Whatever happens in the body influences the mind, and whatever happens in the mind influences the body. Consciousness relies on the body to manifest. Our feelings need to have a body in order to be felt. Without a body, how could we feel? But this doesn't mean that when the body is dead, we disappear. Our body and mind are a source of energy, and when that energy is no longer manifesting in the forms of body and mind, it manifests in other forms: in our actions of body, speech, and mind.

We don't need a permanent, separate self in order to reap the consequences of our actions. Are you the same person you were last year, or are you different? Even in this lifetime, we cannot say that the one who sowed good seeds last year is exactly the same person as the one who reaps the benefit this year.

Unfortunately, many Buddhists still hold on to the idea of a self to help them understand the teachings on reincarnation, karma, and retribution. But this is a very diluted kind of Buddhism, because it has lost the essence of the Buddha's teachings on no self, impermanence, and our true nature of no birth and no death. Any teaching that does not reflect these insights is not the deepest Buddhist teaching. The Three Doors of Liberation— emptiness, signlessness, and aimlessness—embody the cream of the Buddha's teaching.

In Buddhism, if you touch the reality of interbeing, impermanence, and no self, you understand reincarnation in quite a different way. You see that rebirth is possible without a self. Karma is possible without a self, and retribution is possible without a self.

We are all dying and being reborn at every moment. This manifestation of life gives way to another manifestation of life.

We are continued in our children, in our students,
in everyone whose lives we have touched.

"Rebirth" is a better description than "reincarnation." When a cloud turns to rain, we cannot say that a cloud is "reincarnated" in the rain. "Continuation," "transformation," and "manifestation" are all good words, but perhaps the best word is "remanifestation." The rain is a remanifestation of the cloud. Our actions of body, speech, and mind are a kind of energy we are always transmitting, and that energy manifests itself in different forms again and again.

Once a young child asked me, "How does it feel to be dead?" This is a very good, very deep question. I used the example of a cloud to explain to her about birth, death, and continuation. I explained that a cloud can never die. A cloud can only become something else, like rain or snow or hail. When you are a cloud, you feel like a cloud. And when you become rain, you feel like the rain. And when you become snow, you feel like the snow. Remanifestation is wonderful.

CHAPTER 2

SIGNLESSNESS
A CLOUD NEVER DIES

Death is essential to making life possible.
Death is transformation. Death is continuation.

Suppose we look up to the sky and notice a beautiful cloud. We think, "Ah, that's a lovely cloud." Then we look up a few moments later and the sky is clear and blue, and we think, "Oh, the cloud has disappeared." One moment things seem to exist and then they're gone. We look at things this way because we have a tendency to be caught up in signs, appearances, and familiar forms, and this distracts us from seeing the true nature of reality.

When we see something we recognize in the phenomenal world, like a cloud, we say it is there, it exists. And when we can no longer see it, we say it is not there, it no longer exists. But the underlying truth is that it still exists, even if its appearance has changed. The challenge is to recognize that thing in its new forms. This is the meditation on signlessness.

Whether or not we can understand the true nature of birth and death, and overcome fear, grief, anger, and sorrow, depends on whether we can see things with the eyes of signlessness. If we know how to look with the eyes of signlessness, it's not at all difficult to answer the question: What happens when we die?

SIGNLESSNESS: THE SECOND DOOR OF LIBERATION

A sign is what characterizes the appearance of something, its form. If we recognize things based on their sign, we may think that this cloud is different from that cloud, the oak tree is not the acorn, the child is not the parent. At the level of relative truth, these distinctions are helpful. But they may distract us from seeing the true nature of life, which transcends these signs. The Buddha said, "Where there is a sign, there is always deception." With the insight of interbeing we can see there is a profound connection between this cloud and that cloud, between the acorn and the oak, between parent and child.

The cloud that was in the sky earlier may seem to have disappeared. But if we look deeply, we see that the same elements that made up the cloud have now become rain, mist, or even snow. The true nature of the cloud, H_2O, is still there, existing in new forms. It is impossible for H_2O to pass from something into nothing, from being into nonbeing. Although we can no longer see it, the cloud has not died. Perhaps it turned into rain, which then became the water that flowed out of the faucet and into my kettle, filling my cup with tea. The cloud that was in the sky yesterday has not disappeared; it has become tea. It has not died; it is just playing hide-and-seek!

You too are always changing form. You browse through a family photo album and come across a photo of yourself as a young child. Where is that little child now? You know that it is you. You have the same name, and yet it doesn't look like you. Are you still that child or are you someone else? This is a practice of contemplating your own signlessness. Today you look, speak, act, and think differently. Your form, feelings, perceptions, and consciousness are all very different. You are not fixed or permanent. So you are not the same person, but you are not a totally different person either. When you are no longer caught in specific images or appearances, you can see things more clearly. You can see that the little child is still alive in every cell of your body. It is possible to listen to and take care of the little boy or little girl in you at any time. You can invite that child to breathe with you, walk with you, and enjoy nature with you.

YOUR BIRTH DAY

In this very moment all of us are dying. Some of us are dying more slowly and some of us more quickly. If we can be alive now, it is because we're dying at every moment. We might think that some-one else is dying and we're not. But we shouldn't be fooled by appearances.

There are two levels of truth about birth and death. At the level of conventional truth, we can say there is birth and death, begin-ning and ending, creation and destruction. We can, for example, look at a calendar and put in the date of when someone was born and when someone died. Most of us get a birth certificate when we are officially born, without which it is difficult to get a passport or to register for school. And when we die, a death certificate is issued with the date and time of death. In that sense, birth and death are real. They are important. They are useful concepts. But they are not the whole truth.

Looking more deeply, you can see that the moment you were

officially born is not really the moment of your birth. It is only a moment of continuation. Before that, you already existed. You were in the womb for eight or nine months. At what moment did you become you? Some people might say you should move your date of birth to the day you were conceived. But that would not be entirely accurate either. Long before the moment of your conception, the elements you are composed of were already present in the sperm and egg that came together to help you manifest. You also existed in all the conditions that supported and nourished your mother as she was pregnant. And long before that, you were in your grandparents. In fact, you could keep pushing your date of birth back infinitely. There is no moment when you did not exist. This is why in the Zen tradition we ask questions like "What did you look like before your grandmother was born?"

The day you call your birthday is really a day to remember your continuation. Every day you are alive is a continuation day. Within your body, birth and death are always taking place. We are coming into existence and going out of existence at every moment of our life. When you scratch or scrub yourself, dry skin is flaked off and new skin cells are born. In the time it takes you to read this paragraph, thousands of cells will have died. But there are so many, you do not have time to organize funerals for them. At the same time, thousands of new cells have been born, but it would be impossible to organize birth celebrations.

Every day you transform.
Some part of you is being born and some part is dying.

There is an intimate connection between birth and death. Without the one, we cannot have the other. As it says in the gospel, unless the seed dies, it could never bear fruit.

We have a tendency to think of death as something very negative, dark, and painful. But it's not like that. Death is essential to making life possible. Death is transformation. Death is continuation. When we die, something else is born, even if it takes time to reveal itself or for us to be able to recognize it. There may be some pain at the moment of dying, just as there is pain at the moment of birth, or when the first bud bursts through the bark of a tree in spring. But once we know that death is not possible without the birth of something else, we are able to bear the pain. We need to look deeply to recognize the new that manifests when something else dies.

HIDE-AND-SEEK

In my hermitage in France there is a bush of japonica, Japanese quince. The bush usually blossoms in spring. One winter it was very warm and the flower buds came early. But during the night, a cold snap arrived and brought with it frost. The next day while doing walking meditation, I noticed that all the buds on the bush had died. It was very sad to see. The blossoms hadn't even seen the light of day and yet they died.

A few weeks later the weather got warm again, and on my walk I saw new buds on the japonica. They were so beautiful—young and fresh. I was delighted. And I asked them, "Are you the same as the buds that died in the frost or are you different?" The flowers replied, "We are not the same and we are not different. When conditions are sufficient we manifest, and when conditions are not sufficient we go into hiding."

Before my mother gave birth to me, she was pregnant with another baby boy, but she had a miscarriage. When I was young I always wondered: Was that my brother or was it me who was trying to manifest? If a baby has been lost, it means that conditions were not sufficient for them to manifest, and the child has decided to withdraw so they can wait for better conditions. "I had better withdraw; I'll come back again soon, my dearest." We have to respect their will. If you see the world with eyes like this, you will suffer much less. Was it my brother whom my mother lost? Or maybe I was about to come out but instead I said, "It isn't time yet," so I withdrew.

The insight of emptiness and signlessness can help free us from our grief. The little baby has no separate self. The baby is made of the mother, the father, and so many other causes and conditions.

When these elements come together again, the next baby will be neither exactly the same nor different. Nothing is lost.

YOUR LIFE SPAN IS LIMITLESS

When we speak about a "date of birth" or "time of death," these are really just notions. To say we have a "life span" is also just a notion. These labels and signs are conventional designations that are useful at the level of relative truth, but they're not the ultimate truth. They're not the reality. If we're afraid of or angry or sad about death, it's because we're still caught up in our incorrect notions of birth and death. We think death means that from something we will become nothing. But if we see all the ways in which we exist beyond our body, constantly changing forms, we realize nothing is lost. And we no longer feel so angry or afraid.

When a cloud becomes rain, we may be tempted to say that the cloud has died. But we know the cloud's true nature, H_2O, hasn't died at all. It has become rain. If we want to see the true nature of the cloud, we have to free ourselves from the sign "cloud." The dying of a cloud is at the same time the birthing of the rain. If the cloud did not die, how could the rain be born? But the cloud need not wait until that moment in order to see the birth of the rain. Because, like us, the cloud is dying in every moment.

Let's say you heat water in a kettle. As the water heats, some steam already begins to form. There is a more rapid transformation as the temperature rises to one hundred degrees Celsius, and more water transforms into vapor. Evaporation is at once the death of water and the birth of vapor, which will later become a cloud in the sky. The same is true for us. Sometimes there is slow transformation and sometimes there is more abrupt transformation.

We don't need to wait until the water of our own life is nearing one hundred degrees Celsius to see this—by then it may be too late. We should take the time now, while we're still alive, to understand living and dying, in order to free ourselves from anxiety, fear, and sorrow. Whether we're dying quickly or slowly, it's all the same. With this insight, the quality of our life becomes richer, and we appreciate every moment. One day lived deeply with this insight may be worth more than a thousand days without it.

It's the quality of our life that is important,
not how long we live.

ALIVE OR DEAD?

When we look at an oak tree, it may be difficult to imagine that it grew out of an acorn. Is that acorn still alive? If it is, then why can't we see it? Or does the acorn no longer exist? If it died, then how come there is an oak tree now?

The teachings on signlessness help us break free from our tendency to put things into boxes. We usually try to fit life into one of four categories:

1. Is it alive?
2. Is it dead?
3. Is it still in the realm of being? In other words, does it still exist?
4. Has it passed into the realm of nonbeing? Does it no longer exist?

The truth is that we can't fit reality into the categories of "existing" and "not existing." Once we've touched the ultimate truth, we see that the categories of "alive" and "dead" don't apply—whether it's to a cloud, an acorn, an electron, a star, ourselves, or our beloved ones.

Just as we need to liberate ourselves from the idea of a self, or a human being that's different from other living beings, we also need to liberate ourselves from the sign and appearance of a life span. Your life span is not limited to seventy, eighty, or one hundred years, and that is good news. Your body is not your self; you are much more than this body. You are life without boundaries.

YOU ARE MUCH MORE THAN THIS BODY

By now you may already begin to see that we are not limited to our physical body, even while we are alive. We inter-are with our ancestors, our descendants, and the whole cosmos. We don't have a separate self, we are never really born, and we never really die. We are interconnected with all life, and we are always in transformation.

Buddhist traditions have developed many ways to visualize our life without boundaries, and one of those ways is to see that, as well as our human body, we have many other "bodies." Some traditions say we have three; others say five or seven. Looking deeply, understanding the nature of emptiness and signlessness and the insight of interbeing, we can identify at least eight different bodies. When we are able to recognize and experience all our bodies, we live our life more fully and face the disintegration of our physical body without fear.

The word "body" here simply means a collection of energy—a body of energy. Modern science tells us that everything we perceive is energy. Some kinds of energy we can see or detect with our senses, and some we can detect only with specialized instruments. There may also be types of energy we have not yet learned how to measure, but even so, we may be able to feel and perceive them.

We have a close relationship with all our eight bodies. We can take care of them, and they will be there, strong and healthy for us when we need them, and they will encompass the qualities we would like to continue after we pass away.

One of my students said, "If I have eight bodies, then I'm going to have to shower eight times—one time for each body!" But when we see the interconnection between all the eight bodies, we see that we need to shower mindfully only once, and we can save a lot of water.

It's wonderful to have so many bodies. But don't take my word for it. Investigate and see for yourself.

FIRST BODY: THE HUMAN BODY

Thanks to our human body, we can feel, we can heal, and we can transform. We can experience life in all its wonders. We can reach out to take care of someone we love. We can reconcile with a family member. We can speak up for others. We can see something beautiful. We can hear the song of the birds and the voice of the rising tide. And we can act to make our world a healthier, more peaceful, and more compassionate place. Thanks to our body, everything is possible.

And yet a lot of the time many of us completely forget we have a body. Our body is there, but our mind is somewhere else, not with the body. Our mind is alienated from the body. It is with our projects, our worries, our fears. We can work on a computer for hours and completely forget our body, until something starts to hurt. But how can we say we're truly living our life if we've forgotten we have a body? If our mind is not with our body, we cannot say that we're fully present. We cannot say that we're truly alive.

> Breathing mindfully, you simply
> enjoy your in-breath and out-breath.
> You bring the mind home to the body, and you realize
> that you are alive, still alive, and this is a wonder.
> To be alive is the greatest of all miracles.

Most of us still need to learn how to take care of our physical body. We need to learn how to relax and how to sleep. We need to learn how to eat and consume in such a way that our body can be healthy, light, and at ease. If we listen carefully, we can hear our body telling us all the time what it does and does not need. Although its voice is very clear, we seem to have lost our capacity to listen to it. We've pushed our body too hard, and so tension and pain have accumulated. We've been neglecting our body so long, it may be lonely. Our body has wisdom, and we need to give ourselves a chance to hear it.

In this very moment you may like to pause and reconnect with your body. Simply bring your awareness to your breathing, and recognize and acknowledge the presence of your whole body. You may like to say to yourself, "My dear body, I know you are there." Coming home to your body like this allows some of the tension to be gently released. This is an act of reconciliation. It is an act of love.

Our body is a masterpiece of the cosmos. Our body carries within it the stars, the moon, the universe, and the presence of all our ancestors. How many millions of years of evolution has it taken to give rise to these wondrous two eyes, legs, feet, and hands? Countless life-forms are supporting our existence in this moment. Reconnecting with our physical body takes only a few moments of stopping and breathing with awareness. We all have time for this, and yet we do not do it. It is strange that we are scared of what happens to our physical body when we die, and yet we are not truly enjoying our physical body while we are alive.

We have to learn to live our life deeply as a human being.
We need to live every breath deeply,
so that we have peace, joy, and freedom as we breathe.

When we see clearly that our physical body is a miraculous wonder of life, a gift of the cosmos, it is a flash of insight. Once we have that insight, we must sustain it. If not, restlessness and agitation will take over, and we'll forget. We'll no longer cherish the miracle of being alive. So we need to sustain and nurture this insight in every moment. It takes concentration. But it's not hard to do. While we walk, while we work, while we eat, we bring our awareness to our human body, simply enjoying the feel of our body's position and movements, and the wonder of being alive.

But we should not be caught up in thinking that our body is our self. Our body is made entirely of non-body elements, including the four great elements of earth, water, fire, and air. Contemplating these elements, we can see a deep connection between the inside and the outside of our body. We cannot draw a boundary between them. The four elements in us are one with the four elements outside us. Input and output are always taking place. In this very moment we are receiving and releasing water, warmth, and breath; and we can see countless cells and atoms from our body being nourished by and returning to the earth. When we are sick or dying, it can be very helpful to contemplate this. But we don't need to wait until then to do so. We don't return to the earth only when our entire body disintegrates. We return to the earth and we are renewed by the earth at every moment.

SECOND BODY: THE BUDDHA BODY

Having a human body means you also have a buddha body. The word "buddha" means someone who is awakened and who is working for the awakening of other beings. "Buddha body" is just a shorthand way of describing our capacity to be awake and fully present, to be understanding, compassionate, and loving. You don't need to know or use the word "buddha" to have a buddha body. You don't have to believe in anything, not even the Buddha. The Buddha Shakyamuni was not a god. He was a human being with a human body, and he lived in such a way that his buddha body could grow.

Every human being can become a buddha. This is good news. We all have the seeds of mindfulness, love, understanding, and compassion, and whether these good seeds have a chance to grow depends on our environment and our experiences. Don't doubt that you have a buddha body. There have been times in the past when you had the capacity to understand, to forgive, and to love. These are the seeds of your buddha body. You have to give the buddha in you a chance.

Allowing the buddha in you to grow doesn't require special effort. If you wake up to the beauties of nature, you are already a buddha. And if you know how to maintain that spirit of being awake all day, you are a full-time buddha.

It's not so difficult to be a buddha; just keep your awakening alive all day long. We're all capable of drinking our tea in mindfulness. Every one of us can breathe, walk, shower, and eat in mindfulness. Every one of us can wash the dishes in mindfulness. Every one of us can speak and listen with compassion. The more you water the seeds of mindfulness, concentration, insight, and love in you, the more your buddha body will grow, and the happier and freer you'll become. Whatever our livelihood is—whether we're a teacher, an artist, a social worker, or a businessperson—we can participate in the work of a buddha, helping to nurture enlightenment and awakening and to bring positive change to the world. When we can be fully present and get in touch with the wonders of life that have the power to heal and nourish us, we will have enough strength to help others suffer less. Someone who has not woken up cannot help another person to wake up. A non-buddha cannot make another buddha.

To be a buddha—to wake up—also means to wake up to the suffering in the world and find ways to bring relief and transformation. This requires a tremendous source of energy. Your strong aspiration—your mind of love—is that immense source of energy that helps wake you up to the nourishing and healing beauties of nature and to the suffering of the world. It gives you a lot of energy to help. This is the career of a buddha. And if you have that source of strength in you, if you have the mind of love, you are a buddha in action.

THIRD BODY: THE SPIRITUAL PRACTICE BODY

Our spiritual practice body grows from our buddha body. Spiritual practice is the art of knowing how to generate happiness and handle suffering, just as a gardener knows how to make good use of mud in order to grow lotus flowers. Spiritual practice is what helps us to overcome challenging and difficult moments. It is the art of stopping and looking deeply to gain deeper insight. It is very concrete. We cultivate our spiritual practice body—which we can also call our "Dharma body"—by cultivating the seeds of awakening and mindfulness in our daily life. The more solid our spiritual body becomes, the happier we will be and the more we are able to help those around us be happier and suffer less. We all need a spiritual dimension in our life.

It is up to each one of us to develop a strong spiritual practice body every day. Every time you take one peaceful step or one mindful breath, your spiritual practice grows. Every time you embrace a strong emotion with mindfulness and restore your clarity and calm, it grows. Then, in difficult moments, your spiritual practice body will be right there with you when you need it. It is there with you at the airport, in the supermarket, or at work.

People can steal your phone, computer, or money,
but they can never steal your spiritual practice.
It is always there to protect and nourish you.

In the time of the Buddha there was a monk named Vaikali, who had been one of the Buddha's attendants. It so happened that Vaikali was overly fond of the Buddha, and when the Buddha noticed this, he didn't allow Vaikali to be his attendant anymore. This was very painful for Vaikali, and he suffered very much. He even attempted suicide. Vaikali was attached to the Buddha's human body. But with the practice and teachings, he was able to grow and transform, and deepen his understanding of true love.

Then one day, when the Buddha was staying at Rajagriha, the capital of an ancient kingdom in northwest India, he got word that Vaikali was very sick and dying. At this time the Buddha himself was also nearing his own death, but he walked down from Vulture Peak, where he had been staying, and went to visit Vaikali at the house of a potter. The Buddha wanted to speak to Vaikali to see if he was free and ready to release his body without fear. And so he asked, "Dear friend, do you have any regrets?"

"No, dear teacher, I have no regrets," replied Vaikali, "except one: that I'm so sick I can no longer climb the mountain to contemplate you sitting on Vulture Peak." There was still some attachment.

"Vaikali, come on!" exclaimed the Buddha. "You already have my Dharma body. You don't need my human body!" What we have learned from our teachers is far more important than their physical presence. Our teachers have transmitted to us the fruit of all their wisdom and experience. The Buddha was trying to tell Vaikali that he should look for the teacher within, not the teacher outside. Our teachers are there within us. What more could we want?

My physical body may not last very long, but I know that my spiritual practice body, my Dharma body, is strong enough to continue for a very long time. It has helped me through so much. If it were not for my Dharma body, if it were not for my practice of mindfulness, I would never have been able to overcome the great difficulties, pain, and despair I have faced in my life. I have endured wars and violence, my country was divided, my society and Buddhist community were wrought apart, and we encountered so much discrimination, hatred, and despair. It is thanks to my Dharma body that I have been able to survive, and not only survive but overcome all these difficulties, and grow and transform through them.

I do my best to transmit every practice experience I've had to my students. My Dharma body is the best gift I have to offer. It is the body of all the spiritual practices and insights that have brought me healing, transformation, happiness, and freedom. I trust that all my friends and students will receive my spiritual practice body and nourish it even further for the sake of future generations. We need to practice well, and to continue to help our spiritual practice body grow and become more and more appropriate to our time.

FOURTH BODY: THE COMMUNITY BODY

In 1966 I was exiled from Vietnam because I had dared to come to the West and call for peace. I felt like a bee removed from its beehive or like a cell suddenly separated from the body. I was cut off from all my colleagues and friends in Vietnam, who were doing their best to continue our vital social work and educational programs without me. It was a very difficult and painful time. But the practice of mindfulness helped me to heal, and I began to find ways to build a community outside Vietnam.

When I met with Dr. Martin Luther King Jr. for the last time a year later, we spoke about our dreams of building community. He called it the "beloved community." A beloved community is a community of people who share the same aspiration and want to support each other to realize that aspiration. If we want to grow on our spiritual path, we need a community and spiritual friends to support and nourish us. And in return, we support and nourish them, like cells in the same body. On our own, without a community, we cannot do much. We need a community of like-minded friends and colleagues to help us realize our deepest dreams.

> *It is possible to transform not only our home but*
> *also our work, school, corporation, or hospital into a*
> *beloved community, into a kind of family, where there*
> *is love, understanding, and true communication.*

We start with a few colleagues who have the same aspirations, and we build up from there. Four people is enough. Five is good. And more than five is excellent.

The key elements in a beloved community are love, trust, joy, harmony, and brotherhood and sisterhood. When we can generate understanding and compassion in our way of being and working together, everyone we interact with feels that energy right away and is able to profit from it. We can create moments to listen deeply to one another's insights and difficulties, or a relaxing moment with tea and cookies where we take time just to be fully present for each other. Our community can become a source of support and a place of refuge for many people. We nourish our community in our lifetime, and it carries us forward into the future.

FIFTH BODY: THE BODY OUTSIDE THE BODY

Each one of us can be present in many places in the world. We can be here and at the same time in a prison. We can be here and also in a distant country where the children suffer from malnutrition. We don't have to be present with our physical body. When I write a book, I transform myself into thousands of me that can go a little bit everywhere. Every book becomes my body outside the body.

I can enter a home in the form of one of my calligraphies.
I can go to a prison in the form of a DVD.

One time, when I was teaching in Madrid, Spain, a woman from South America told me about a mental health clinic that had programmed a bell of mindfulness to play over its PA system. A bell of mindfulness is a bell that reminds us to stop and come home to ourselves. Every time the doctors, nurses, and patients heard the bell, they would stop what they were doing, come back to themselves, relax, and enjoy breathing mindfully. The clinic also programmed mindfulness bells to sound on its computers and phones. This woman reported that it had a very calming, positive effect on all the healthcare professionals and patients. I have often suggested that it is possible to create moments of stopping, calming, and true presence in health-care environments, but I have never been to this clinic, nor have our Dharma teachers. How is it possible that none of us has ever been there yet they practice stopping with the bell the same way we do in all our mindfulness practice centers? Our presence, our practices and actions, are non-local. I am not just this flesh and these bones weighing several dozen kilos.

In many prisons in North America and the United Kingdom there are inmates who practice walking and sitting meditation. They have learned to breathe, to walk, and to speak with kindness and compassion. These prisoners are also me. They are my body, because they have read my books; they are practicing what they have read and are continuing me. They are my body outside my body.

One prisoner happened to have the book *Stepping into Freedom*, the manual I wrote for training novice monks and nuns, and after reading it, he wanted to become a novice monk. Realizing it would be impossible for anyone to ordain him, he shaved his own head and transmitted to himself the precepts that a teacher normally would pass on to a student. Then he practiced as a novice monk in his cell in the prison. When I hear these kinds of stories, I know that I am everywhere and my community body is everywhere. Our body is non-local. That prisoner who is practicing mindful walking is us. Our body is not only here; our body is there. We are present everywhere at the same time.

It is the same for a father and son, or a mother and daughter. When a father looks at his son with the eyes of signlessness, he sees that his son is also himself. He is the father, but he is also the son. When a father looks like that, he can see his body outside his body. When the child looks at his father and sees himself in his father, he sees his body outside his body. When looking at our children or grandchildren, we see ourselves, and we begin to see our body outside this body.

SIXTH BODY: THE CONTINUATION BODY

Throughout our life we produce energy. We say things and do things, and every thought, every word, and every act carries our signature. What we produce as thoughts, as speech, as action, continues to influence the world, and that is our continuation body. Our actions carry us into the future. We are like stars whose light energy continues to radiate across the cosmos millions of years after they become extinct.

When you produce a thought of hatred, anger, or despair, it harms you, and it also harms the world. None of us wants to be continued like that. We all want to produce thoughts of compassion, understanding, and love. When you are able to produce a thought of compassion and understanding, it is healing and nourishing for yourself and the world. Just as an acidic cloud produces acid rain, so will the energy of anger, fear, blaming, or discrimination produce a toxic environment for ourselves and others. Use your time wisely. Every moment it is possible to think, say, or do something that inspires hope, forgiveness, and compassion. You can do something to protect and help others and our world.

We have to train ourselves in the art of right thinking so we can produce positive, nourishing thoughts every day. If you had a negative thought about someone in the past, it's not too late to do something about it. The present moment contains both the past and the future. If today you can produce a thought of compassion, of love, of forgiveness, then that positive thought has the power to transform the negative thought of yesterday and to guarantee a more beautiful future tomorrow.

> *Every day we can practice producing thoughts*
> *of compassion. Thinking is already action.*
> *Every compassionate thought bears our signature.*
> *It is our continuation.*

Our words are energy that has a ripple effect far beyond our imagining. We must learn the art of communicating so our speech can bring about love, reconciliation, and understanding. Just as it tastes bitter to utter words that are negative or unkind, it feels wonderful to say something full of understanding and love. Reconciling with someone we're angry with, using loving speech, is healing for both parties. Straightaway we feel lighter and at peace. Challenge yourself. Practice mindful breathing, deep breathing, and see the suffering in yourself and in the other person. Then, resolve to call him or her and produce one or two minutes of right speech. We may have been waiting a long time to do this. Perhaps they have been waiting for us too, without even knowing it.

Perhaps instead of calling, you can write an email or a text message that is full of understanding and compassion. Healing already takes place, even before you send it. It is never too late to reconcile with a loved one, even if they have already passed away. You can still write them a letter, expressing your regrets and love. This alone will bring about peace and healing. Your words can be beautiful gems, reaching across space and time to create mutual understanding and love.

We are also continued in our bodily actions. Whenever we do something with our physical body that protects, helps, saves, or inspires someone else, that act is also nourishing and healing for us and for the world. We need to ask ourselves: "Where am I investing my physical energy?" "What will I leave behind when my body disintegrates?" "What can I do today to realize my dreams?"

Let's look again at the cloud in the sky. While the cloud is still a cloud, she can already begin to see her continuation body in the form of rain, snow, or hail. Let's say one-third of the cloud has become rain and the other two-thirds of the cloud is still up in the sky, happily watching the rain falling down to earth. She is seeing her continuation body. To be a cloud is beautiful. But to be rain falling down and becoming a stream of water is also beautiful. The cloud enjoys looking down from the sky and seeing her continuation body as a fresh, clear stream of water meandering through the countryside.

When I was eighty years old, a journalist asked me if I ever planned to retire as a spiritual teacher. I smiled and explained that teaching is given not by talking alone but by the way we live our life. Our life is the teaching. Our life is the message. And so I explained that as long as I continue to practice mindful sitting, walking, eating, and interacting with my community and those around me, I will continue to teach. I told her that I had already started encouraging my senior students to begin to replace me by giving their own Dharma talks. Many of them have given wonderful Dharma talks, and some have been better than mine! When they teach, I see myself continued in them.

When you look at your son, your daughter, or your grandchildren, you can see that they are your continuation. When a schoolteacher looks at their class, they can see their students as their continuation. If they are a happy schoolteacher, if they have a lot of freedom, compassion, and understanding, their students will also be happy and feel understood. It is possible for each of us to see our continuation right away. This is something we have to remind ourselves to do every day. When I look at my friends, students, and the more than one thousand monks and nuns I have ordained, who are practicing mindfulness and leading retreats around the world, I see my continuation body.

Even if we are still very young, we already have
a continuation body. Can you see it?

Can you see how you are continued in your parents, in your brothers and sisters, in your teachers and friends? Can you see the continuation body of your parents and loved ones? We don't need to get old or die in order to see our continuation body. We don't need to wait for the complete disintegration of this body in order to begin to see our continuation body, just as a cloud doesn't need to have been entirely transformed into rain in order to see her continuation body. Can you see your rain, your river, your ocean?

Each one of us should train ourselves to see our continuation body in the present moment. If we can see our continuation body while we're still alive, we'll know how to cultivate it to ensure a beautiful continuation in the future. This is the true art of living. Then, when the time comes for the dissolution of our physical body, we will be able to release it easily.

I sometimes liken my body to the water being boiled in a kettle that eventually turns to steam. When my body disintegrates, you may say "Thich Nhat Hanh has died." But this is not true. I will never die.

My nature is the nature of the cloud—the nature of no birth and no death. Just as it's impossible for a cloud to die, it's impossible for me to die. I enjoy contemplating my continuation body, just as the cloud enjoys watching the rain fall and become the river far below. If you look closely at yourself, you will see how you too are continuing me in some way. If you breathe in and out, and you find peace, happiness, and fulfillment, you know I am always with you, whether my physical body is still alive or not. I am continued in my many friends, students, and monastic disciples. I am continued in the countless people all over the world whom I have never met but who have read my books, listened to one of my talks, or practiced mindfulness with a local community or in one of our practice centers. If you look with the eyes of signlessness, you will be able to see me far beyond this body.

So the shortest answer to the question "What happens when I die?" is that you don't die. And that is the truth, because when you understand the nature of the person who is dying, and you understand the nature of the act of dying, you will see there is no such thing as death anymore. There is no self who dies. There is only transformation.

SEVENTH BODY: THE COSMIC BODY

Our cosmic body encompasses the entire phenomenal world. The wonder that is our human body will disintegrate one day, but we are much more than this human body. We are also the cosmos, which is the foundation of our body. Without the cosmos, the body could not be here. With the insight of interbeing we can see that there are clouds inside us. There are mountains and rivers, fields and trees. There is sunshine. We are children of light. We are sons and daughters of the sun and stars. The whole cosmos is coming together to support our body in this very moment. Our little human body contains the entire realm of all phenomena.

We can visualize our human body as a wave, and our cosmic body as all the other waves on the ocean. We can see ourselves in all the other waves and all the other waves in us. We don't need to go looking for our cosmic body outside us. It is right here within us at this very moment. We are made of stardust. We are children of the Earth, made of all the same elements and minerals. We contain mountains, rivers, stars, and black holes. In every moment of our life the cosmos is going through us, renewing us, and we are returning ourselves to the cosmos. We are breathing the atmosphere, eating the earth's food, creating new ideas, and experiencing new feelings. And we are emitting energy back into the cosmos, in our thinking, speech, and actions, in our out-breath, in our body's warmth, and in releasing everything we have consumed and digested. In this very moment many parts of us are returning to the earth. We don't return to the earth and cosmos only when our body disintegrates.

We are already inside the earth, and the earth is inside us.

Our human body is a masterpiece of the cosmos, and when we treasure, respect, and cherish our body, we are treasuring, respecting, and cherishing our cosmic body. When we live in such a way that we take good care of our body, we are taking care of our ancestors and we are taking care of our cosmic body.

EIGHTH BODY: THE ULTIMATE BODY

Our eighth body is the deepest level of the cosmic: the nature of reality itself, beyond all perceptions, forms, signs, and ideas. This is our "true nature of the cosmos" body. When we get in touch with everything that is—whether it is a wave, sunshine, forests, air, water, or stars—we perceive the phenomenal world of appearances and signs. At this level of relative truth, everything is changing. Everything is subject to birth and death, to being and nonbeing.

But when we touch the phenomenal world deeply enough, we go beyond appearances and signs to touch the ultimate truth, the true nature of the cosmos, which cannot be described in notions, words, or signs like "birth" and "death" or "coming" and "going."

We are a wave appearing on the surface of the ocean. The body of a wave does not last very long—perhaps only ten to twenty seconds. The wave is subject to beginning and ending, to going up and coming down. The wave may be caught in the idea that "I am here now and I won't be here later." And the wave may feel afraid or even angry. But the wave also has her ocean body. She has come from the ocean, and she will go back to the ocean. She has both her wave body and her ocean body. She is not only a wave; she is also the ocean. The wave does not need to look for a separate ocean body, because she is in this very moment both her wave body and her ocean body. As soon as the wave can go back to herself and touch her true nature, which is water, then all fear and anxiety disappear.

The deepest level of our consciousness, which we call "store consciousness," has the capacity to directly touch the ultimate— the realm of reality itself. Our mind consciousness may not be able to do that right now, but our store consciousness is touching the true nature of the cosmos, in this very moment.

As you get in touch with your cosmic body, it's as though you stop being a block of ice floating on the ocean and you become the water. With our mindful breathing and deep awareness of our body, we are able to leave the zone of cogitating, discriminating, and analyzing, and enter the realm of interbeing.

EVERYTHING INTER-IS

There is a deep connection between all our different bodies. Our physical body, our buddha body, our spiritual practice body, our body outside the body, our continuation body, and our cosmic body inter-are. Our human body contains both our cosmic body and the true nature of the cosmos—reality itself, beyond all words, labels, and perceptions. Our cosmic body is the universe, creation, the masterpiece of God. Looking deeply into the cosmos, we see its true nature. And we can say that the true nature of the cosmos is God. Looking deeply into creation, we see the creator.

At first it seems as though things exist outside one another. The sun is not the moon. This galaxy is not another galaxy. You are outside me. The father is outside the son. But looking deeply, we see that things are interwoven. We cannot take the rain out of the flower or the oxygen out of the tree. We cannot take the father out of the son or the son out of the father. We cannot take anything out of anything else. We are the mountains and rivers; we are the sun and stars. Everything inter-is. This is what the physicist David Bohm called "the implicate order." At first we see only "the explicate order," but as soon as we realize that things do not exist outside one another, we touch the deepest level of the cosmic. We realize that we cannot take the water out of the wave. And we cannot take the wave out of the water. Just as the wave is the water itself, we *are* the ultimate.

Many still believe that God can exist separately from the cosmos, his creation. But you cannot remove God from yourself; you cannot remove the ultimate from yourself. Nirvana is there within you.

If we want to touch the ultimate,
we have to look within our own body and not outside.

Contemplating deeply the body from within, we can touch reality in itself. If your mindfulness and concentration are deep as you practice walking meditation in nature, or as you contemplate a beautiful sunset or your own human body, you can touch the true nature of the cosmos.

When we practice mindfulness, we can get many kinds of relief. But the greatest relief and peace comes when we are able to touch our nature of no birth and no death. This is something doable. It's something possible. And it gives us a lot of freedom. If we are in touch with our cosmic body, our God body, our nirvana body, then we are no longer afraid of dying. This is the cream of the Buddha's teaching and practice. There are those who can die happily, in peace, because they have touched this insight.

PRACTICE: CONTEMPLATING LIMITLESS LIFE

It is possible to live your daily life in such a way that you are aware of all your different bodies and feel connected to them every day. You will be able to see your continuation across time and space and realize that your life is limitless. This physical body, which will disintegrate one day, is only a small part of who you are.

You may like to take a moment to contemplate the following text. It is an invitation to see that you are life without boundaries; you are life without limit. You can read it slowly, allowing each line to fall like gentle rain on the soil of your consciousness.

I see that this body—made of the four elements—is not really me, and I am not limited by this body. I am the whole of the river of life, of blood ancestors and spiritual ancestors, that has been continuously flowing for thousands of years and flows on for thousands of years into the future. I am one with my ancestors and my descendants. I am life manifesting in countless different forms. I am one with all people and all species, whether they are peaceful and joyful or suffering and afraid. At this very moment I am present everywhere in this world. I have been present in the past and will

*be there in the future. The disintegration of this body
does not touch me, just as when the petals of the plum
blossom fall it does not mean the end of the plum tree.
I see that I am like a wave on the surface of the ocean.
I see myself in all the other waves, and I see all the other
waves in me. The manifestation or the disappearance of
the wave does not lessen the presence of the ocean.
My Dharma body and spiritual life are not subject to birth
or death. I am able to see my presence before this body
manifested and after this body disintegrates. I am able
to see my presence outside this body, even in the present
moment. Eighty or ninety years is not my life span. My life
span, like that of a leaf or of a buddha, is immeasurable.
I am able to go beyond the idea that I am a body separate
from all other manifestations of life, in time and in space.*

GUIDED MEDITATION:
BREATHING WITH THE COSMOS

Breathing in, I see the element earth in me, the element air in me.
I see clouds, snow, rain, and rivers in me. I see the atmosphere,
wind, and forests in me, the mountains and oceans in me. I see the
earth in me.

Breathing out, I smile to the earth in me. I am one with Mother Earth, the most beautiful planet in our solar system.

> *Mother Earth in me.*
> *Smiling to the most beautiful planet in our solar system.*

Breathing in, I see the element of light in me, I am made of light; I am made of the sun. I see our star as an infinite source of life, nourishing us in every moment. Buddha Shakyamuni was a child of Father Sun; so too am I.

Breathing out, I smile to the sun in me. I am the sun, a star, one of the most beautiful stars in our entire galaxy.

> *I am a child of the sun.*
> *I am a star.*

Breathing in, I see all my ancestors in me: my mineral ancestors, plant ancestors, mammal ancestors, and human ancestors. My ancestors are always present, alive in every cell of my body, and I play a part in their immortality.

Breathing out, I smile to the cloud in my tea. A cloud never dies. A cloud can become snow or rain but never nothing. I also play my part in the immortality of the cloud.

I am my ancestors.
Playing my part in the immortality of my ancestors.

Breathing in, I see the stars and galaxies in me. I am conscious-ness manifesting as cosmos. I am made of stars and galaxies.

Breathing out, I smile to the stars in me. I play my part in the immortality of clouds, rain, stars, and the cosmos.

Smiling to the stars and galaxies in me.
Playing my part in the immortality of stars and cosmos.

Breathing in, I see that nothing is created, nothing is destroyed; everything is in transformation. I see the nature of no birth and no death of matter and energy. I see that birth, death, being, and nonbeing are only ideas.

Breathing out, I smile to my true nature of no birth and no death. I am free from being and from nonbeing. There is no death; there is no fear. I touch nirvana, my true nature of no birth and no death.

Nothing is created. Nothing is destroyed.
I am free from being, free from nonbeing.

CHAPTER 3

AIMLESSNESS
RESTING IN GOD

You already are what you want to become.
You are a marvel. You are a wonder.

One day the Buddha was visited by a strident deity on horseback called Rohitassa, who saw himself as something of a hero.

"Dear teacher," he asked, "do you think it's possible to escape this world of birth and death, suffering and discrimination, by means of speed?" It seems humans have always had a desire to travel quickly, to get places fast. Even now we dream of building machines that can travel at the speed of light, hoping to visit other dimensions. In the Buddha's time there were no airplanes or space rockets. The fastest you could travel was on the back of a horse.

The Buddha replied gently, "No, Rohitassa, it is not possible to escape this world by traveling, even at great speed."

"Right you are!" said Rohitassa. "In a previous life I traveled extremely fast, as fast as the speed of light. I didn't eat, didn't sleep, didn't drink. I did nothing but travel at great speed, and still I could not get out of this world. In the end I died before I could do so. So I quite agree, it's impossible!"

"But, my friend," continued the Buddha, "there *is* a way to get out. You only need to look inside. Looking deeply into your own body, barely six feet tall, you can discover the immensity of the cosmos. You can touch your true nature beyond birth and death, suffering and discrimination. You don't need to go anywhere."

Many of us have been running all our lives. We have the feeling that we need to run—into the future, away from the past, out from wherever we are. In truth, we don't need to go anywhere. We just need to sit down and look deeply to discover that the whole cosmos is right here within us. Our body is a wonder containing all kinds of information. To understand ourselves is to understand the whole cosmos.

The way out is in.

So long as we think we are a separate self distinct from the world around us, we think we can get out of the world. But once we see that we *are* the world, that we are made entirely of non-us elements, we realize that we do not need to go running after anything outside of us. The world cannot get out of the world. We already are everything we are looking for.

RESTING IN GOD

Just as a wave doesn't need to go looking for water, we don't need to go looking for the ultimate. The wave *is* the water. You already *are* what you want to become. You are made of the sun, moon, and stars. You have everything inside you.

In Christianity there is the phrase "resting in God." When we let go of all seeking and striving, it is as if we are resting in God. We establish ourselves firmly in the present moment; we dwell in the ultimate; we rest in our cosmic body. Dwelling in the ultimate doesn't require faith or belief. A wave doesn't need to *believe* it is water. The wave is already water in the very here and now.

To me, God is not outside us or outside reality. God is *inside*. God is not an external entity for us to seek, for us to believe in or not believe in. God, nirvana, the ultimate, is inherent in every one of us. The Kingdom of God is available in every moment. The question is whether we are available to it. With mindfulness, concentration, and insight, touching nirvana, touching our cosmic body or the Kingdom of God, becomes possible with every breath and every step.

AIMLESSNESS:
THE THIRD DOOR OF LIBERATION

The concentration on aimlessness means arriving in the present moment to discover that the present moment is the only moment in which you can find everything you've been looking for, and that you *already are* everything you want to become.

Aimlessness does not mean doing nothing. It means not putting something in front of you to chase after. When we remove the objects of our craving and desires, we discover that happiness and freedom are available to us right here in the present moment.

We have a habit of running after things, and this habit has been transmitted to us by our parents and ancestors. We don't feel fulfilled in the here and now, and so we run after all kinds of things we think will make us happier. We sacrifice our life chasing after objects of craving or striving for success in our work or studies. We chase after our life's dream and yet lose ourselves along the way. We may even lose our freedom and happiness in our efforts to be mindful, to be healthy, to relieve suffering in the world, or to get enlightened. We disregard the wonders of the present moment, thinking that heaven and the ultimate are for later, not for now.

To practice meditation means to have the time to look deeply and see these things. If you feel restless in the here and now, or you feel ill at ease, you need to ask yourself: "What am I longing for?" "What am I searching for?" "What am I waiting for?"

THE ART OF STOPPING

We have been running for thousands of years, and that is why it is difficult to stop and encounter life deeply in the present moment. Learning to stop may sound easy, but in fact it takes training.

I remember one morning contemplating a mountain in the early light of dawn. I saw very clearly that not only was I looking at the mountain, but all my ancestors in me were looking at the mountain with me. As dawn broke over the mountain peak we admired its beauty together. There was nowhere to go and nothing to do. We were free. We needed only to sit there and enjoy the sunrise. Our ancestors may never have had a chance to sit quietly, peacefully, and enjoy the sunrise like that. When we can stop the running, all our ancestors can also stop at the same time. With the energy of mindfulness and awakening, we can stop on behalf of all our ancestors. It is not the stopping of a separate self alone, but of a whole lineage.

As soon as there is stopping,
there is happiness. There is peace.

When we stop like that, it looks as if nothing is happening, but in fact everything is happening. You are deeply established in the present moment, and you touch your cosmic body. You touch eternity. There is no more restlessness, no more seeking.

In Plum Village, and in all our mindfulness practice centers in the United States, Europe, and Asia, we practice stopping every time we hear the sound of a bell. Whether it is the great temple bell, the clock chiming in the dining hall, the bells of the surrounding village churches, or even the sound of the telephone—as soon as we hear the sound of the bell, we take a moment simply to stop, relax, and breathe. We come back to ourselves and to the present moment. If we're talking, we stop talking. If we're walking, we stop walking. If we're carrying something, we put it down. We return to our breathing and arrive in our body in the here and now. We relax and just enjoy listening to the sound of the bell.

Listening to the bell, we enter into a deep relationship with the present moment that embraces limitless time and limitless space. The past and the future are right here in the present moment. God, nirvana, the cosmic body, are available. The moment becomes an eternal, fulfilled moment.

Where is your father, your mother, your grandfather or grandmother? Right here in the present moment. Where are your children, grandchildren, and future generations? Where are Jesus Christ and the Buddha? Where are love and compassion? They are here. They are not realities independent from our consciousness, from our being, from our life. They are not objects of hope or pursuit outside of us. And where is heaven, the Kingdom of God? Also right here. Everything we are looking for, everything we want to experience, has to happen right here in the present moment. The future is merely an idea, an abstract notion.

Only the present moment is real.

If we continue to hold on to a dream for something in the future, we lose the present moment. And if we lose the present, we lose everything. We lose freedom, peace, joy, and the opportunity to touch the Kingdom of God, to touch nirvana.

The Gospel of Matthew tells the story of a farmer who discovers treasure hidden in a field and returns home to sell everything he has so he can buy the field. That treasure is the Kingdom of God, which is found only in the present moment. You need only one moment of awakening to realize that what you are looking for is already there, in you and around you. Like the farmer, as soon as we discover this, we can easily let go of everything else in order to touch true peace, happiness, and freedom in the present moment. It's worth it. To lose the present moment is to lose our only chance to encounter life.

THE CYPRESS IN THE COURTYARD

There is a Zen story about a student who felt he hadn't really received the deepest essence of his master's teaching, and so he went to question him. His master replied, "On your way here, did you see the cypress in the courtyard?" Perhaps the student was not yet very mindful. The master was saying that if, on the way to see our teacher, we go past a cypress tree or a beautiful plum tree in blossom and we don't really see it, then when we arrive in front of our teacher, we won't see our teacher either. We shouldn't miss any opportunity to really see our cypress tree. There are wonders of life we walk past every day, and yet we haven't truly seen them. What is the cypress tree on the path you take to work every day? If you cannot even see the tree, how can you see your loved ones? How can you see God?

Every tree, every flower belongs to the Kingdom of God. If the dahlia in bloom does not belong to the Kingdom of God, where does it belong? If we want to have a relationship with God, if we want to understand God, all we need to do is behold the cypress tree on our path.

Mindfulness helps us arrive in the present moment to see and hear the wonders of life—to see and hear God.

If there is a spiritual crisis in the twenty-first century, it is that we have not put God in the right place, namely within ourselves and in the world around us. Can you take God out of the cosmos? Can you take the cosmos out of God?

We are a wonder, and we are surrounded by wonders. We have God, we have the cosmic body, we have everything right in this moment. With this insight, with this kind of enlightenment, we already feel happy, content, and fulfilled.

HEAVEN ON EARTH

For some of us, our highest dream is to go to a heaven or, if we are Buddhist, to a "Pure Land" after we die. We believe this life is somehow insufficient and unsatisfactory and that we can touch only the deepest, most fulfilling level of existence after we die. We feel we need to shed this body in order to truly touch the ultimate. We have a sense that there must be a better place, a happier, more perfect place, somewhere else, later on.

But if we wait until we die to expect happiness, it may be too late. We can touch all the wonders of life, and the ultimate itself, with our human body right here and now. Your body is also a wonder. It is another kind of flower in the garden of humanity, and you should treat your body with the utmost respect because it belongs to the Kingdom of God. You can touch the Kingdom of God with your body. One mindful in-breath is enough for us to suddenly notice the bright blue sky, the cool fresh air, the sound of the wind in the pine trees, or the music of the running brook. We don't need to die to go to heaven. We already are in the Kingdom of God.

BE BEAUTIFUL; BE YOURSELF

We may be able to see the wonders around us and yet still doubt that we ourselves are a wonder too. We feel inadequate. We're yearning for something else, something more. We are like a saucepan wandering around looking for a lid. We lack confidence in ourselves and in our capacity to be peaceful, compassionate, and awakened. We feel overwhelmed by our difficulties. And so we continue to go about our daily life feeling that we lack something. We've got to ask ourselves, "What am I lacking? What am I looking for?"

To practice aimlessness is to identify what it is you're looking for, waiting for, or running after, and let it go. By removing these objects of seeking that are pulling you away from the here and now, you will discover that everything you want is already right here in the present moment. You don't need to "be someone" or do something in order to be happy and free. If you ask a flower blooming on the mountainside, or a tree standing majestically in the forest, "What are you looking for?," how would they reply? If you have some mindfulness and concentration, you will hear their answer in your heart.

Each one of us has to be our true self:
fresh, solid, at ease, loving, and compassionate.
When we are our true selves, not only do we benefit,
but everyone around us profits from our presence.

YOU ARE ENOUGH

The renowned ninth-century Chinese Zen master Lin-Chi taught that "humans and buddhas are not two," and declared, "There is no difference between you and the Buddha!" He was saying that you are already enough. We don't need to do anything special to be a buddha and cultivate our buddha body. We just need to live a simple, authentic life. Our true person, our true self, doesn't need a particular job or position. Our true self doesn't need money, fame, or status. Our true self doesn't need to do anything. We just live our life deeply in the present moment. When we eat, we just eat. When we wash the dishes, we just wash the dishes. When we use the bathroom, we just enjoy using the bathroom. When we walk, we just walk. When we sit, we just sit. Doing all these things is a wonder, and the art of living is to do them in freedom.

*Freedom is a practice and a habit. We have to train
ourselves to walk as a free person, sit as a free person, and
eat as a free person. We need to train ourselves how to live.*

The Buddha also ate, walked, and went to the toilet. But he did so in freedom, not rushing from one thing to the next. Can we live like that? Can we use our time just to live true to ourselves? If we are still seeking or pursuing something else, something more, we're not yet aimless. We're not yet free, and we're not yet our true self. Our true self is already there within us, and as soon as we can see it, we become a free person. We have been free from beginningless time. We just need to be able to recognize it.

I once had a chance to visit the Buddhist Ajanta Caves in the state of Maharashtra in India. They are entirely carved out of the mountain rock. There are living quarters, with holes dug out for monks to put their alms bowls and sanghati robes in. The day I visited it was very hot, and I lay down to enjoy the pleasant coolness and freshness of the cave.

Nothing was brought from the outside to make those caves. The temples were simply dug out of the rock. The more rock they removed, the larger the caves became. Touching our true self, our true nature, is like that. All the things we think we've got to find on the outside are already there inside us. Loving-kindness, understanding, and compassion are there within us. We need only to clear some of the rock obstructing the way in order to reveal them. There is no essence of holiness we need to seek outside. And there is no essence of the ordinary we have to destroy. We already are what we want to become. Even in our most difficult moments, everything that is good, true, and beautiful is already there, within us and around us. We just have to live in such a way that allows it to be revealed.

BEING BUSINESS-LESS

Master Lin-Chi exhorted his students to be "business-less." It means to not be getting busy all the time, to be free from busyness. If we can be business-less, we can touch the spirit of aimlessness in our daily life, not being carried away by our desires, plans, and projects. We don't do things to get praise or status; we don't try to play a role. Wherever we are, we can be sovereign of ourselves. We're no longer swept away by our environment; we're no longer pushed or swayed by the crowd.

Whatever we are doing,
we can do it with ease and freedom.

For Master Lin-Chi, the ideal life is not to be an enlightened "arhat" or a "bodhisattva" devoted to serving all beings, but to be a business-less person. A person who is business-less has realized the insights of emptiness, signlessness, and aimlessness. They are not caught in the idea of a self, they have no need for the "signs" of fame or status, and they dwell freely and happily in the present moment.

To be business-less is to live our daily life in touch with the ultimate dimension. In the ultimate dimension, there is nothing to do. We already are what we want to become. We are relaxed; we are at peace. There is no need to run anymore. We are happy and free from worry and anxiety. This is the way of being that is most needed in the world. It is very pleasant to dwell in the ultimate dimension, and we should all learn how to do it.

"But," you may ask, "if we are happy in the present moment, with nowhere to go and nothing to do, then who will help living beings become liberated? Who will rescue those who are drowning in the ocean of suffering? Does being aimless make us indifferent to the suffering in the world? If our priority is to be free and happy, doesn't that paralyze us, and lead us to avoid the challenges and difficulties of trying to help others?"

The Buddha was no longer looking or yearning for anything, no longer striving, and yet he was someone who never ceased to help liberate all beings. Throughout the forty-five years of his ministry, he continued to help liberate others from their suffering, even to the last moments of his life. Being aimless doesn't mean we are without compassion and loving-kindness. As soon as we have compassion, loving-kindness, and understanding, we naturally have a strong motivation to act and to help.

What's essential is to bring a different quality of being to the situation of suffering in the world. If we are suffering just like everyone else, how can we help them suffer less? If doctors have the same sickness as their patients, how can they help them heal?

Our energy of peace, joy, compassion, and freedom is essential. We have to nourish and protect our way of being. Whatever we do needs to have a spiritual dimension.

When our work and life has a spiritual dimension,
we're able to sustain ourselves, take care
of ourselves, and avoid burning out.

In the 1960s I wrote the book *The Miracle of Mindfulness* as a manual for the thousands of young social workers who were being trained in our School of Youth for Social Service in Vietnam. The intention was to help them practice so they could stay healthy, focused, and compassionate, so they could nourish their aspiration and have enough joy and peace to continue their work of service.

It is possible to work, serve, and engage as a free person without getting lost in our work. We don't miss out on the present moment striving or struggling to achieve a future goal—we live deeply each moment of our work. This is the meaning of aimlessness. The peace, freedom, compassion, and loving-kindness we radiate already helps those around us to suffer less. We are not passive. To be passive means to be pulled, pushed, and swayed by circumstances or the people around us. But our freedom and sovereignty means that we don't become a victim of circumstances.

With compassion and insight, we ask ourselves, "In this situation, what can I do to stop things getting worse? How can I help the situation improve?" When we know that we are doing our best on the path of relieving suffering, it is possible to be at peace every step along the way.

BEING AND DOING

My name, Nhat Hanh, means "one action." I spent a long time trying to find out which action this was. Then I discovered that my one action is to *be* peace and to bring peace to others.

We have a tendency to think in terms of doing and not in terms of being. We think that when we're not doing anything, we're wasting our time. But that's not true. Our time is first of all for us to *be*. To be what? To be alive, to be peaceful, to be joyful, to be loving. And this is what the world needs the most. We all need to train ourselves in our way of being, and that is the ground for all action.

Our quality of being determines our quality of doing.

There are those who say, "Don't just sit there—do something!" When we see injustice, violence, and suffering all around us, we naturally want to do something to help. As a young monk in Vietnam in the 1950s and '60s, together with my friends and students, we did everything we could to create a grassroots Buddhism that could respond to the enormous challenges and suffering of the times. We knew that offering chants and prayers was not enough to save the country from the desperate situation of conflict, division, and war.

We began publishing a large national weekly Buddhist magazine, started the School of Youth for Social Service to bring relief and support to villages devastated by the war, and also founded Van Hanh University in Saigon to offer a more modern approach to education for the young generation. In all this work, we learned that the quality of our action depended on the quality of our being. So every week we organized a whole day of mindfulness practice at the nearby Bamboo Forest Monastery. There we practiced sitting meditation, walking meditation, and mindful eating together, and we took time to listen deeply to one another's challenges and joys. With the energy of brotherhood and sisterhood, we created a wonderful, happy place of refuge.

So as well as saying, "Don't just sit there—do something!" we can also say, "Don't just do something—sit there!" Stopping, being still, and practicing mindfulness can bring about a whole new dimension of being. We can transform our anger and anxiety, and cultivate our energy of peace, understanding, and compassion as the basis for action. The energies of wisdom, compassion, inclusiveness, fearlessness, patience, and non-discrimination—never disparaging anyone—are all the qualities of awakened beings. Cultivating these energies helps us bring the ultimate dimension into the historical dimension, so we can live a life of action in a relaxed and joyful way, free from fear, stress, and despair. We can still be very active but do everything from a place of peace and joy. This is the kind of action that is most needed. When we can do this, the work we do will be of great help to ourselves and the world.

THE ACTION OF NON-ACTION

Sometimes, not doing anything is the best thing we can do. Non-action is already something. There are people who do not seem to do very much, but their presence is crucial for the well-being of the world. There may be someone in our own family who does not make a lot of money, and we could say they are not very active, but if that person wasn't there, the family would be much less happy and stable because that person is contributing the quality of their being, their non-action.

Imagine a boat of desperate refugees crossing the ocean. The boat gets caught in a storm and everyone panics. If everyone panics, there's a high chance they will do the wrong thing and the boat will capsize. But if just one single person can remain calm, they will be able to inspire others to be calm. If, from a place of peace, they ask everyone to sit quietly, the whole boat can be saved. That person doesn't exactly do anything. What they contribute above all is their calmness and the quality of their being. That is the action of non-action.

As a society we are always striving to do things to resolve the many difficulties we face. And yet it seems that the more we do, the worse the situation gets. So we have to look into the ground of our actions, which is our quality of being.

In Plum Village we have organized retreats for Israelis and Palestinians. Back in the Middle East, their lives may be a daily struggle to survive. There is always something to do and not a moment to stop. But when they come to Plum Village, we create a peaceful environment for them to rest, stop, sit quietly, and come back to themselves. They just sit with us, walk with us, and eat with us. They practice deep relaxation. No one is doing anything special, yet it is already a revolution. After only a few days of practice, they feel a lot better. They have space inside, and they are able to sit there and listen to the suffering of the other side with compassion. Many young people on these retreats have told us that it was the first time in their lives that they believed peace was possible in the Middle East.

If we want to organize a peace conference or a conference on the environment, we can do it in the same way. World leaders can come together, not merely to sit around a table and make decisions, but to spend time together as friends and establish a human relationship. When we can listen deeply to each other's suffering and difficulties, and when we can express our insights and ideas using loving speech, then our negotiations will be successful. Once there is understanding, releasing fear and anger becomes possible.

*Restoring communication is the most
basic practice for peace.*

We have to organize so there is enough time to live together peacefully, think peacefully, and act peacefully during the conference, in order to give rise to the kind of insight that our nations need. Peace is not something to hope for in the future. Peace is something that we can *be* in every moment. If we want peace, we have to be peace. Peace is a practice and not a hope. We say that our leaders can't afford to spend one or two weeks together like this, and yet war and violence are costing us so much money and so many lives. Our political leaders need the help of spiritual leaders to address these global problems. They have to work hand in hand. True peace work requires a spiritual dimension—the practice of peace.

WHAT IS YOUR DREAM?

I was once asked by a journalist in Holland, "Do you have anything left you want to do before you die?" I didn't know how to answer her, because she was not very familiar with the teachings. So the best I could do was simply to look at her and smile.

The truth is I really don't feel that there is anything I have to do before I die, because the way I see it, I won't ever die. And the things I want to do, I've been doing for a long time already. In any case, in the ultimate dimension, there is nothing more to do. As a thirty-year-old monk during the war in Vietnam, I wrote a poem with the lines "Dear ones, the work of rebuilding may take thousands of lifetimes, but this work was already completed thousands of lifetimes ago." In the ultimate dimension, there is nothing for us to do. To practice aimlessness doesn't mean that we don't have a dream or aspiration. It means to stay in touch with the ultimate dimension in the present moment, so we can realize our dreams with joy, ease, and freedom.

Every one of us has a deep desire to realize something in our lifetime. Whether or not you are aware of it, deep in your heart there is something you've always wanted to accomplish. Not just a fleeting wish but a deep intention that may have begun to grow in your heart while you were still very young. This is your dearest dream, your ultimate concern. When you identify and nurture your deepest desire, it can become a source of great happiness, energy, and motivation. It can provide you with drive, with direction. It can sustain you through difficult moments.

Our dream gives us vitality. It gives our life meaning.

Everyone has a dream. You need to take the time to be still, to look deeply, and to listen to your heart to find out what your deepest desire is. Is it to have a lot of money, power, fame, or sex, or is it something else? What do you really want to do with your life? You should not wait until you are already old to ask yourself these questions. Once you can identify your deepest intention, you have a chance to be true to yourself, to live the kind of life you'd like to live, and to be the kind of person you'd like to be.

SHARED DREAMS

When you start a relationship with someone, you also need to find out what their deepest dreams are. You need to ask them what they want to do with their life. You need to discover this before you get married, not afterward. If you live with someone but each of you is pursuing a different ideal, you'll never be able to relate to each other deeply. So you need to take time to sit down with your partner and ask these questions. If you love them, you need to understand them, and you also need to help them understand you. It is tragic to share a bed yet dream different dreams. Talking with your partner about your dreams is a way to deepen communication and connection so you can both go in the same direction together.

You can also ask your parents about their dreams. "Did you ever have a dream when you were young? Were you able to realize it?" If you can ask questions like this, your relationship with your parents will become real and deep. It's a way to discover who your parents really are. It will enable them to open their hearts, and you will feel as close to them as a good friend. And if your parents have not yet been able to realize their dream, you may be able to realize it for them, because you are their continuation.

Looking into your body, your feelings, and your suffering, you can see the body, the suffering, and the hopes and dreams of your parents. Even if your parents have already passed away, you can look deeply into these questions and hear the answers, because you are your parents' continuation, and they are still alive within you, in every cell of your body.

The same is true of your spiritual ancestors. Even if you have never met them, if you have received their teachings and put them into practice, then they too are alive in you. They are present in the way you take a mindful step, in the way you break the bread.

SURRENDER

A student once asked me what I thought it meant to "surrender to God's will." For me, God's will is that each of us should be our best. We should be alive, and we should enjoy the wonders of life and do our best to help others do the same. That is the will of God. It is also the will of nature. Mother Earth is always doing her best to be as beautiful and fresh as she can be, to be as accepting and forgiving as she can be. Mother Earth is doing God's will. And we, who are children of the Earth, can learn from her. We can learn to be as patient and tolerant as she is. We can live in such a way that we cultivate and preserve our freshness, beauty, and compassion.

If we have the good intention to cultivate happiness, to transform our suffering, and to help those around us transform theirs; if we have the intention to be fully present, to live deeply the life that has been given to us, and to help others do the same, that is surrendering to the will of God. It is not a passive kind of surrender. The will to live peacefully, happily, and with compassion is full of vitality. And it's not only the will of God; it's also our own will. So the one who surrenders and the one who is surrendered to are not separate entities. The ultimate is right here within us.

YOUR DREAM IS NOW

We have the tendency to think there is a means, a path, to realizing our dream, and that we realize our dream at the end of the path. But in the spirit of Buddhism, as soon as you have a dream, an intention, an ideal, you have to live it. Your dream can be realized right in the present moment. You live your life in such a way that every step in the right direction and every breath along the way becomes the realization of your dream. Your dream does not take you away from the present; on the contrary, your dream becomes reality in the present moment.

Living each moment as a way to realize our dreams,
there is no difference between the end and the means.

For example, let's say you dream of liberation, enlightenment, and happiness. In your daily life all your thoughts, words, and deeds should be directed toward realizing liberation, enlightenment, and happiness. You do not need to wait until you have come to the end of your path to have these things. As soon as you take a step toward liberation, liberation is already there. Liberation, enlightenment, and happiness are possible each step of the way. There is no way to happiness; happiness is the way.

YOUR DESTINATION IS IN EVERY STEP

A few years ago I visited the Wutai Shan Mountain in China with a number of monastic students and friends. It's a popular destination for pilgrims and tourists, and is said to be the dwelling place of Manjushri, the Bodhisattva of Great Understanding. There were over a thousand steps leading up the mountain, but our aim was not to get to the top. Our aim was to touch peace and joy with every step.

I remember the walk very clearly. I breathed in as I took one step up, and breathed out as I took the next step. Many people were huffing and puffing as they overtook us, and they turned around to look back and see who was going so slowly. We enjoyed every single step. And from time to time we stopped to enjoy the view. When we arrived at the top of the mountain we were not tired at all. We were full of energy, completely refreshed and nourished by the climb.

When human beings first developed the capacity to walk and run it was either to chase after something or to escape something. That energy of chasing and running is deeply ingrained in every cell of our body. But today there is no longer the same need to hunt, fight, or escape from danger, and yet we still walk with that kind of energy. We have developed from *Homo erectus* to *Homo sapi-*

ens, and now we have a chance to become *Homo conscius*—a mindful, awakened species. This species will learn to walk in freedom. Walking in peace and freedom is a wonderful way to bring the ultimate dimension into the historical dimension. It's a way to train ourselves not to run.

PRACTICE: THE ART OF WALKING

You may like to apply the practice of mindful walking wherever you go, in the city or in a park, going to work or going shopping, at the airport or by the bank of a river. Nobody needs to know you are practicing walking meditation. You walk naturally and at ease. I suggest you choose a short distance that you walk every day, perhaps from the parking lot to the office or from your home to the bus stop. It doesn't take a long time to master walking meditation. We can feel the benefit right away. A single step is enough to touch peace and freedom.

Walking meditation is linked to the practice of mindful breathing. When you walk, you coordinate your breathing and your steps. Relax your body and let go of any thinking about the past and the future, and bring your mind back to the present moment. Feel the contact with the ground. As you breathe in, notice the number of steps you are making while breathing in. As you breathe out, notice the number of steps that you are making while breathing out. Allow your breathing to be natural, and simply pay attention to how many steps you take as you breathe in and out. After a while, you notice there is a rhythm, a coordination, between your breathing and your steps. It's like music.

Concentrating a hundred percent on our breath liberates us.
We become a free person in just a few seconds,
free to transform the habits of our ancestors.

When you practice mindful walking, you walk with your body and your mind together. You should really be there, fully present in every step. "I am here. I am really here." You might like to try slow walking. If you're alone, you can be as slow as you want. When you breathe in, just take one step. And when you breathe out, just take one step.

While breathing in, you might like to say, "I have arrived." While breathing out, you can say, "I am home." It means, I have arrived in the present moment, in the here and the now. This is not a declaration; it's a realization. You have to really arrive. Every step helps you to stop running—not only your body but also the running of your mind. With walking meditation, you recognize your habit of running so you can gradually transform it.

You need to invest one hundred percent of your body and mind in walking meditation so you can truly arrive. This is a challenge. If you cannot arrive now, when will you arrive? So stay there. Continue to breathe until you feel that you have completely arrived, that you are totally present. Then you can make another step and imprint the seal of arrival on the ground. Smile a smile of victory and rejoice! The entire cosmos is witness to your arrival. If you can make one step like this, you can make two or three. What's essential is that you succeed in making the first step.

"I have arrived; I am home" means "I don't want to run anymore." I've been running all my life and I've arrived nowhere. Now I want to stop. My destination is the here and now, the only time and place where true life is possible.

This is slow walking meditation—a way to truly train yourself in really stopping, calming, and arriving. Once you've mastered the art of walking slowly, you'll be able to practice walking meditation at any speed. Walking mindfully doesn't necessarily mean walking slowly. It means walking with peace and freedom. Each step taken in mindfulness nourishes and heals you. You simply go home to your breathing and your body. With every breath, with every step, you allow your body and your feelings to relax. You walk naturally, in peace and freedom, fully present in every step, aware of your body and everything all around you.

With every step you have sovereignty, you have freedom, you are your true self. You don't need to get to your destination in order to arrive. You arrive at every step. You realize that you are alive and that your body is a masterpiece of the cosmos. As you touch peace and freedom in every step, you are touching nirvana, your cosmic body, your God body. Don't think that nirvana is something far away. You can touch nirvana at every step.

When we practice walking meditation we
touch the ultimate, the Kingdom of God, with
our feet, our mind, and our whole body.

CHAPTER 4

IMPERMANENCE
NOW IS THE TIME

Thanks to impermanence, everything is possible.

There are turtles that live to be three or four hundred years old, and redwood trees that live more than a thousand years. Our own life span is only about a hundred years at most. How are we living those years? Are we making the most of our days? What are we here to realize or to accomplish?

Later, we may look back and wonder, "What have I done with my life?" Time goes by so quickly. Death comes unexpectedly. How can we bargain with it? To wait until tomorrow is too late.

We all want to live deeply so our lives are not wasted and when death comes we won't have any regrets.

When we are fully established in the present moment, we know that we are alive, and that it's a miracle to be alive. The past has gone, and the future has not yet come. *This* is the only moment where we can be alive, and we have it!

We have to make this present moment into
the most wonderful moment of our life.

Contemplating impermanence helps us touch freedom and happiness in the present moment. It helps us see reality as it is, so we can embrace change, face our fears, and cherish what we have. When we can see the impermanent nature of a flower, a pebble, the person we love, our own body, our pain and sorrow, or even a situation, we can make a breakthrough into the heart of reality.

Impermanence is something wonderful. If things were not impermanent, life would not be possible. A seed could never become a plant of corn; the child couldn't grow into a young adult; there could never be healing and transformation; we could never realize our dreams. So impermanence is very important for life. Thanks to impermanence, everything is possible.

WE'LL SEE, WE'LL SEE

There's an old story from China about Mr. Ly, a rural villager whose livelihood depended on his horse. One day his horse ran away, and all his neighbors took pity on him: "How unlucky you are! What misfortune!" But Mr. Ly was not anxious. "We'll see," he said. "We'll see."

A few days later his horse returned, bringing several wild horses back with it. Mr Ly and his family were suddenly very wealthy. "How lucky you are!" exclaimed the other villagers. "We'll see," replied Mr. Ly. "We'll see." Then one day his only son was training one of the new wild horses and he fell off and broke his leg. "What misfortune!" declared the neighbors again. "We'll see," said Mr. Ly. "We'll see."

A few weeks later the imperial army passed through the village, to conscript all able-bodied young men into the military. They did not take away Mr. Ly's son, who was still recovering from his broken leg. "How lucky you are!" said his neighbors again. "We'll see," replied Mr. Ly. "We'll see."

Impermanence is just as capable of bringing about happiness as it is of bringing about suffering. Impermanence is not bad news. Because of impermanence, despotic regimes are subject to fall.

Because of impermanence, illness can be cured. Thanks to impermanence, we can enjoy the wonder of the four beautiful seasons. Thanks to impermanence, anything can change and transform in a more positive direction.

There were times during the war in Vietnam when it seemed the violence would never end. Our teams of young social workers labored tirelessly to rebuild villages that had been destroyed by bombs. So many people lost their homes. There was one village near the demilitarized zone that we had to rebuild not only one but two and even three times after repeated bombings. The young people asked, "Should we rebuild? Or should we give up?" Luckily, we were wise enough not to give up. To give up would be to give up on hope.

I remember that about this time a group of young people came to me and asked, "Dear teacher, do you think the war will end soon?" At that point, I could not see any sign of the war ending. But I did not want us to drown in despair. I stayed silent for some time. Finally, I said, "Dear friends, the Buddha said that everything is impermanent. The war has to end one day." The question is, what can we do to accelerate the impermanence? There are always things we can do each day to help the situation.

THE POWER OF INSIGHT

We may agree with the truth of impermanence, and yet we still *behave* as though everything is permanent, and that is the problem. This is what prevents us from taking the opportunities available to us right now to act to change a situation, or to bring happiness to ourselves and others. With the insight of impermanence, you won't wait. You'll do everything you can to make a difference, to make the person you love happy, and to live the kind of life you would like to live.

The Buddha offered the contemplation on impermanence not for us to treasure as a notion, but for us to get the *insight* of impermanence by applying it to our daily life. There's a difference between a notion and an insight.

Say we strike a match to get a flame. As soon as the flame manifests, it begins to consume the match. The notion of impermanence is like the match, and the insight of impermanence is like the flame. As the flame manifests, it consumes the match, which we don't need anymore. What we need is the flame, not the match. We're making use of the notion of impermanence to get the *insight* of impermanence.

*We can make the insight of impermanence into a
living insight that is with us in every moment.*

The insight of impermanence has the power to liberate us. Suppose someone you love has just said something that has made you angry, and you want to punish them by saying something unkind back. He has dared to make you suffer, and you want to lash back and make him suffer too. You are about to start an argument. But then you remember to close your eyes and contemplate impermanence. You imagine your beloved three hundred years from now. He will be nothing but ash. It may not take three hundred years; perhaps within thirty or fifty years you will both be ash. You suddenly realize how foolish it is to be angry and to argue with each other. Life is so precious. It takes only a few seconds of concentration to recognize and touch your nature of impermanence. The insight of impermanence burns away the anger. And when you open your eyes, you don't want to argue anymore. You just want to hold him in your arms. Your anger has transformed into love.

LIVING IN THE LIGHT OF IMPERMANENCE

Many of the people I have loved in the world—my family members and close friends—have already passed away. That I can still breathe is a miracle, and I know that I breathe for them. Every day when I get up, I stretch my body and do some gentle morning exercises, which brings me a lot of happiness.

I don't exercise to get fit or be healthier;
I do it to enjoy being alive.

The happiness and joy of practicing mindful movements nourishes my body and mind. With each movement I do, I feel how wonderful it is that I can still do it. Exercising like this, I enjoy having a body; I enjoy being alive. I accept life and my body just as it is, and I feel so much gratitude. Even as we age and experience ill health or pain, we can still profit from the moments when the pain is not too strong. If you can still breathe, it's possible to enjoy your breathing. If you can still walk, it's possible to enjoy your walking. If you can get in touch with the elements of peace and freshness within you and around you, both body and mind will benefit, and it will help you embrace the difficulties and pain in your body.

We may fear dying, and yet we find it hard to imagine growing old. We cannot believe that one day we might not be able to walk or stand. If we are lucky, one day we will be old enough to sit in a wheelchair. Contemplating this, we value every step and know that in the future it will not be like it is now. Recognizing impermanence allows us to cherish the days and hours that are given to us. It helps us value our body, our loved ones, and all the conditions that we have for happiness in this moment. We can be at peace knowing we are living our life to the fullest.

BREATHE—YOU ARE ALIVE

I treasure the days and hours I have left to live.
They are so precious,
I vow not to waste a single one.

I have been practicing not wasting a single moment. Whether I'm walking or working, teaching or reading, drinking tea or eating a meal with my community, I treasure every moment. I have been living every breath, every step, and every action, deeply. Wherever I walk, I combine these words with each step. As I breathe in I say, "Breathing legendary breaths," and as I breathe out I say, "Living legendary moments, wonderful moments." Happiness is there at every step, and I know that tomorrow I will have no regrets.

Breathing is a kind of celebration, celebrating
the fact of being alive, still alive.

FACING SILENT FEARS

Often the joy of knowing that we are still alive contains within it the deep fear that we don't want to face: our fear of dying. Although we don't want to admit or think about it, deep down in our hearts we know that one day we will die. The day will come when we will be laid out, our body stiff. We will no longer be able to breathe, we will no longer be able to think, we will no longer have any emotions or feelings, and our body will begin to decompose. We may be uneasy every time we think about death. We may have a tendency to brush it aside. We may be in denial. This fear may be silently haunting us, driving our thoughts, words, and actions without us knowing it.

Maintaining awareness in our daily life of our eight different bodies helps us transform our deeply rooted fear of dying. We see that our physical body is just a tiny part of who we are, and we see all the many ways in which we are being continued. We should not be in denial about our physical body's impermanence. Keeping this awareness alive in our daily life can help us see clearly how to make good use of the time we still have. The Buddha taught the Five Remembrances—a contemplation to recite at the end of every day—as an exercise to lessen our fear of death and remind us of the preciousness of life.

PRACTICE: THE FIVE REMEMBRANCES

You may like to take a moment to read these lines very slowly, with a pause to follow your breathing and relax between each remembrance.

I am of the nature to grow old.
There is no way to escape growing old.

I am of the nature to have ill health.
There is no way to escape ill health.

I am of the nature to die.
There is no way to escape death.

All that is dear to me and everyone I
love are of the nature to change.
There is no way to escape being separated from them.

My actions are my only true belongings.
I cannot escape the consequences of my actions.
They are the ground upon which I stand.

To see the ultimate dimension of reality, we have to look deeply into the historical dimension, the dimension in which we're living. The Five Remembrances help us understand the "relative truth" of death: our body *does* experience ageing, ill health, and death. But we also have our cosmic body, and it's very important to remember that. And the more we look with the insight of signlessness, the more we see that "transformation" is a much better word than "death." As we contemplate impermanence and no self with the fourth remembrance, we start to touch the deeper level of reality, the "ultimate truth" beyond signs. Although death may seem to separate us from those we love, looking deeply we can see that they always continue to be with us in new forms. With the fifth, we remember that our actions continue us into the future, and doing so we touch our true nature of no birth and no death, no coming and no going, no sameness and no difference. Reciting the Five Remembrances regularly helps us apply the insights of emptiness, signlessness, aimlessness, and impermanence in our daily life.

APPLIED INSIGHT

Antoine-Laurent Lavoisier, the father of modern chemistry, is the French scientist who discovered that "nothing is created, nothing is destroyed, everything is in transformation." I sometimes wonder if Lavoisier was able to live his daily life in accordance with this truth. Lavoisier lived at the time of the French Revolution, and at the age of fifty he was killed at the guillotine. He had a wonderful wife who loved him very much and became a scientist too. But, I wonder, if Lavoisier, who had this deep insight that nothing can be destroyed, was afraid of dying the day he walked up to the guillotine?

The insight and discoveries that Lavoisier made in his lifetime continue to resonate to this day. So Lavoisier has not died. His wisdom is still there. He continues in new forms. When we say that nothing is created, nothing is destroyed, everything transforms, this also applies to your body, your feelings, your perceptions, your mental formations, your consciousness.

IMPERMANENCE AND NO SELF

When you touch impermanence deeply, you touch no self. Impermanence and no self are not two different things. In terms of time, it's impermanence, and in terms of space, it's no self, emptiness, interbeing. They are different words, but they are the same thing. The deeper we understand impermanence, the deeper we can understand the teachings on no self and interbeing.

Impermanence is a noun describing the nature of something— whether it's a flower, a star, your loved one, or your own body. But we shouldn't think that impermanence happens only to the outer appearance, and that inside there is something everlasting. Impermanence means that nothing can remain the same thing in two consecutive moments. So in fact there is no lasting "thing" that we can call impermanent; it's semantically absurd to say "everything is impermanent." The truth is that everything *is* only for one brief instant.

Suppose we contemplate the flickering flame of a candle. At first, it seems that there is one continuous flame, but in fact what we are seeing is a multitude of flames succeeding each other. From one millisecond to the next, new flames are manifesting from new non-flame elements, including oxygen and fuel. And the flame is radiating light and heat in all directions. Input and output are going on all the time. The flame we see now is not exactly the same as the flame we saw a moment ago, nor is it entirely different. In the same way, we too are always changing. Our body, feelings, perceptions, mental formations, and consciousness are changing from one moment to the next. Every second, the cells in our body, as well as our feelings, perceptions, ideas, and states of mind, are giving way to new ones.

I remember one time, during a retreat we led in Germany, a young couple got married. The next day, I suggested they ask each other, "My dear, are you the same person I married yesterday, or are you different?" Because according to impermanence, we change from one day to the next. We are not exactly the same person, but we're not exactly a different person either. The me yesterday is different from the me today.

When we fall in love, we have a tendency to want to grasp and keep hold of the one we love. We want them to stay the same forever, and we want them to love us forever. Today, they say we're attractive and they love us, but tomorrow, will they still say "I love you"? When we love someone, we're always afraid of losing them. Our mind is always wanting to hold on to something permanent, something everlasting. We want to stay a certain way, and we want our loved one to stay a certain way. But that's not possible. We are both changing all the time. When we can embrace impermanence, we allow each other to change and grow. From one day to the next, we are neither the same nor different. And this is good news.

*In this moment you are new and your loved one
is new, and that is why you are both free.*

WATERING SEEDS

When we are aware that our loved one is not a separate self but a composition of many elements, we can water the positive elements in them to help them grow. This is true for ourselves as well. We can practice watering the seeds in us that we want to grow and transform. Our mind is like a garden in which there are all kinds of seeds: seeds of joy, peace, mindfulness, understanding, and love, but also seeds of craving, anger, fear, hate, and forgetfulness. How you act and the quality of your life depends on which seeds you water. If you plant tomato seeds in your garden, tomatoes will grow. In the same way, if you water a seed of peace in your mind, peace will grow. When the seed of happiness in you is watered, your happiness will bloom. When the seed of anger in you is watered, you will become angry. The seeds that are watered frequently will grow strong, so you need to be a mindful gardener, selectively watering those seeds you would like to cultivate and not watering the seeds you do not want to grow.

Each one of us has our strengths and weaknesses. We might think "I have a short temper" or "I'm a good friend, I'm a good listener." We believe these qualities define us. But they do not belong to us alone. They belong to the whole stream of our inheritance. When we see that we are made of non-us elements, it is much easier to accept all our good qualities, as well as weaknesses and shortcomings, with understanding and compassion.

When you are in a committed relationship, you have two gardens: your garden and the garden of your beloved. First, you have to take care of your garden and master the art of gardening. In each one of us there are flowers and there is also garbage. The garbage is the anger, fear, discrimination, and jealousy within. If you water the garbage, you will strengthen the negative seeds. If you water the flowers of compassion, understanding, and love, you will strengthen the positive seeds. What you grow is up to you.

If you don't know how to practice selective watering in your own garden, then you won't have enough wisdom to help water the flowers in the garden of your beloved. In cultivating your own garden well, you also help to cultivate your beloved's garden. Even a week of practice can make a big difference. Everyone can do this. We all need to practice like this in order to keep our relationships alive. Every time you practice walking mindfully, investing your mind and body in every step, you help to cultivate the peace, joy, and freedom you need. Every time you breathe in and know you are breathing in, every time you breathe out and smile to your out-breath, you become who you truly are. You become your own master, and the gardener of your own garden.

Take good care of your garden so you can help
your beloved take good care of theirs.

If you are in a difficult relationship and you want to make peace with the other person, you have to go home to yourself first. You have to go home to your garden and cultivate the flowers of peace, compassion, gratitude, understanding, and joy. Only then can you come to the other person and offer patience, acceptance, understanding, and compassion.

When you commit to another person, you make a promise to grow together. It is your responsibility to take care of each other. Yet over time, you may encounter difficulties and you may begin to neglect your garden. One morning, you may wake up and suddenly realize that your garden is overgrown with weeds and that the light has faded from your love. It's never too late to do something about it. Your love is still there, and the person you fell in love with is still there, but your garden is in need of some attention.

IS YOUR LOVE STILL ALIVE?

When you look at your closest relationship, you may feel you can no longer recognize the person you once fell in love with—they seem to have disappeared or turned into someone completely different. Everything has changed. Difficulties and misunderstandings have arisen. Perhaps neither of you has been skillful enough in your way of thinking, in your way of speaking and behaving, and you have neglected your relationship. Through your thoughts or unskillful words and actions, you've unintentionally hurt each other so often that you no longer look at or talk to each other in a loving way. You've made each other suffer too much. It may seem that the love you once shared has gone. But just as the acorn is still there in the oak tree, the love of yesterday is still present today. It is always possible to revive your relationship and rediscover the person you once loved.

Looking with the eyes of signlessness, you will see
the person you once fell in love with is still there.

A middle-aged couple in France once came to visit me in Plum Village and told me their story. When they were first together, they were deeply in love and wrote each other the sweetest and most tender love letters. In those days it was very special to receive a letter in the mail. People listened eagerly for the postman's footsteps in case he had a letter for them. Everyone treasured their love letters and kept them in a safe place so they could be read over and over again. This particular lady stored all her love letters in a cookie tin—a typical French LU biscuit box—which she stored away in her wardrobe.

When we first fall in love, all we want to do is look the other person in the eyes and feel their presence close to us. We don't need to eat or drink or even sleep. Just looking into their eyes is enough to survive on.

But if we don't know how to take care of our love or nurture our relationship, before long we don't feel pleasure looking at our loved one anymore. On the contrary, just looking at them makes us suffer. We would rather check our phone for messages or watch television, even if we don't particularly like what is on, because it's still better than switching off the TV and being confronted with the reality of the other's presence.

This was the case for the French couple. Over the years their love had faded. One day the man had to go away on a business trip and was gone for a few days. It was not the first time, and his partner accepted it with some indifference. Then one morning, while she was spring-cleaning her wardrobe, she came upon the LU box with all their old love letters.

Curious, she opened up the box and began to read one. His words were so sweet and tender and went straight to her heart. Over the years the positive seeds of their love had somehow been covered over with layers of dust and mud, but now, as she reread the letters, the good seeds were again watered in her consciousness. She could hear the love and kindness in her partner's voice. So she read another letter and then another. She sat there and read all the letters in the box—dozens of letters. It was as though fresh rain had begun to fall on her dry, parched soil. She wondered what had become of their beautiful love, of all those happy days together. She remembered that she used to write him love letters too. She used to be able to speak to him so tenderly, with love, acceptance, and understanding.

Having read all the letters, she felt a strong desire to reconnect with the person she fell in love with all those years ago. So she sat down, took out a pen and paper, and wrote to him. She was able to use the same tender and sweet language as in the past. She reminded him of the many beautiful times they had spent together, of their special, intimate connection, and expressed her wish to renew and refresh their love. She put the letter in an envelope and left it on his desk.

A few days later, her partner called to let her know he would have to extend his trip. She replied with such trust and love in her voice he was startled. "If you need a few more days, darling, please stay. But try to come back as soon as you can." It had been years since she had spoken to him in such a kind tone of voice.

When he got home, he found her letter on his desk. He stayed there silently a long time. All the good seeds that had lain dormant for so long were watered as he read her letter. When he came out of the room to greet her, he was a different person. Her gentle, compassionate, and loving words had softened and opened his heart toward her again. After such a long time, he felt seen, appreciated, and loved. Reconciliation had taken place, and they were able to rediscover each other, renew their relationship, and revive their love.

THANKS TO IMPERMANENCE, EVERYTHING IS POSSIBLE

Love is something alive, and it needs to be nourished. No matter how beautiful our love is, if we don't know how to nourish it, it will die. We need to learn how to cultivate our love's garden so that our love story can become a long love story. Don't think that your love has died. The person you fell in love with has not disappeared. They are still there, waiting to be rediscovered.

Life is precious. You are alive now, and you should not miss the opportunity to restore and refresh your love. Mindfulness can produce miracles. When you can recognize your loved one's wonderful qualities and you can feel and express your gratitude, when you can communicate using loving speech and deep listening, you will be able to restore your love and rediscover the beauty in your relationship. Later, when you turn into rain, you will have no regrets.

The truth is that suffering and happiness inter-are; there cannot be one without the other. It is thanks to overcoming difficult moments in our relationships that we can deepen our love. And the good news is that suffering and happiness are both impermanent. That is why the Buddha continued to practice even after he had attained enlightenment; he continued to make good use of suffering to create happiness. It is possible for us all to make good use of suffering to create happiness, just as a gardener makes good use of compost to make flowers.

Our suffering is impermanent,
and that is why we can transform it.
And because happiness is impermanent,
that is why we have to nourish it.

CHAPTER 5

NON-CRAVING
YOU HAVE ENOUGH

*As soon as we realize that in this very moment
we already have enough, and we already are
enough, true happiness becomes possible.*

The art of happiness is the art of living deeply in the present moment. The here and now is the only time and place where life is available and where we can find everything we are looking for, including love, freedom, peace, and well-being.

Happiness is a habit. It's a training. With mindfulness, concentration, and insight, we can free ourselves from feelings of restlessness and craving, and realize that, right now, we already have more than enough conditions to be happy. This is the contemplation on non-craving. Practicing mindful breathing and coming back to ourselves to take care of our body throughout the day, we can free ourselves from our regrets about the past and worries about the future, and live deeply every moment, getting in touch with the wondrous, re-freshing, and healing elements that are available inside and around us.

HOOKED

Contemplating non-craving is another way to practice the concentration on aimlessness. Each one of us has a big block of craving inside. We're always looking outside ourselves for something to make us feel satisfied and complete—whether it is food, sensual pleasures, money, a relationship, social status, or success. But so long as we have the energy of craving in us, we're never satisfied with what we have and with who we are right now, and true happiness is not possible. The energy of craving sucks us into the future. We lose all our peace and freedom in the present moment and feel we can't be happy until we've got what we're craving.

But even if you do get the object of your craving, you never feel truly fulfilled. Like a dog chewing on a bare bone, no matter how many hours you gnaw at your craving, you never feel satisfied. You never feel that you have enough.

*Infatuation can become a kind of prison preventing
us from touching true happiness and freedom.*

We may spend our lives chasing after wealth, status, influence, and sensual pleasures, thinking they will improve the quality of our life. And yet we end up not having any time left to live. Our life becomes just a means to make money and become "someone."

The Buddha used the image of a fish biting on an attractive bait. The fish doesn't know that there's a hook hidden in the bait. It looks so delicious, but as soon as the fish bites, it gets hooked and caught. The same is true with us. We run after things that seem very desirable—like money, power, and sex—without realizing the danger in them. We destroy our body and mind chasing after these things, and yet still we continue chasing them. Just as there's a hook hidden in the bait, there is danger hidden in the object of our craving. Once we can see the hook, whatever it is we're craving simply won't be appealing anymore, and we'll be free.

At first we think that if we let go of what we're craving, we'll lose a lot. But when you finally release it, you see that you have not lost anything after all. You are even richer than before, because you have your freedom, and you have the present moment, just like the farmer who sold everything in order to buy the treasure in the field.

INSIGHT SETS YOU FREE

Every one of us has insight. We know that the object of our craving isn't worth it. We know we don't want to get hooked. We know we don't want to spend all our time and energy on it. And yet we can't let go. This is because we don't know how to apply our insight.

We need to take time to stop and reflect deeply on our situation to identify what it is we're craving. And then we have to identify the hook. What is the danger? What is the suffering hidden in it? We've got to see all the ways in which running after and craving these things has made us suffer.

Every desire has its root in our original, fundamental desire to survive. In Buddhism we don't speak of original sin. We speak of that original fear and desire that manifested in us during our birth and in the precarious moment we took our first, painful breath. Our mother could no longer breathe for us. It was difficult to inhale; we first had to expel water from our lungs. But if we couldn't breathe on our own, we would die. We made it; we were born. And with that birth, our fear of dying was born along with the desire to survive. And as infants, that fear stayed with us. We knew that in order to survive, we had to get someone to take care of us. We may have felt powerless, and we found all sorts of ways to figure out how to get someone else to protect us, take care of us, and ensure our survival.

Even though we have grown into adults, our original fear and desire are still alive. We fear being alone or abandoned; we fear getting old. We crave connection and someone to take care of us. If we work nonstop, it may be because of our original fear that otherwise we cannot survive. And our own fear and desire may come from our ancestors' original fear and desire. They suffered from hunger, wars, exile, and so on, and over thousands of years have endured countless difficulties where survival was touch and go.

When fear, craving, or desire comes up, we need to be able to recognize it with mindfulness and smile to it with compassion. "Hello, fear; hello, craving. Hello, little child; hello, ancestors." Following our breathing, and in the safe island of the present moment, we transmit the energy of stability, compassion, and non-fear to our inner child and our ancestors.

Mindfulness can only help reduce our stress
and tension if it provides us with insight.

Meditation isn't just a temporary place of refuge to help you stop suffering for a while. It's much more than that. Your spiritual practice has the power to transform the roots of your suffering and transform the way you live your daily life. It is insight that helps us calm our restlessness, stress, and craving. Perhaps we can start to speak of "insight-based stress reduction."

YOU ARE FREE TO BE YOURSELF

There's a funny story about something that happened many years ago in a psychiatric hospital in Vietnam. A patient there was very afraid of the chickens that roamed freely in the hospital yard. Every time he saw a chicken, he ran away. One day the nurse asked him, "Why do you keep doing that?" The young man explained that he thought he was a seed of corn, and he was afraid the chickens would eat him. So the doctor summoned him to his office and said, "Young man, you are a human being. You are not a grain of corn. Look, you have eyes, a nose, a tongue, a body, just like me. You're not a grain of corn. You're a human being." And the young man agreed.

So the doctor asked him to write down repeatedly on a sheet of paper, "I'm a human being. I'm not a grain of corn." The young man filled up many sheets of paper with these lines. It seemed he was making a lot of progress. Every time the nurse came to ask him, "Who are you? What are you?" he'd always say, "I'm a human being. I'm not a grain of corn." The doctors and nurses were very happy. They gave him a final appointment with the doctor before he was to be discharged.

As he was walking to the doctor's office for that appointment, he saw a chicken. And he ran away, very fast. The nurse had a hard time catching up with him. Finally, she reached him, and said, exasperated, "What are you doing? Why did you run away? You have been doing so well. You *know* you're a human being. You *know* you're not a grain of corn." The young man answered, "Yes, *I* know very well that I'm a human being and not a grain of corn. But the chicken doesn't know that."

Many of us do things only for the sake of form. We do things not because we believe it's important, but because we think others think it's important. We may even chant or pray or invoke the Buddha's name because we think it matters to the Buddha, but not because it's meaningful for us. The same is true with chasing after signs of success, wealth, or status. We may do it, not because we think it's important, but because we think others expect it of us. But when we truly see the cost of these pursuits, and the hook in them, we won't want to keep running after them anymore. We make use of the insight that we are *already* enough. We don't have anything to prove.

TRUE HAPPINESS

Our quality of life and true happiness does not depend on external conditions or external proof. It doesn't depend on how much money we have, or what kind of job or car or house. In Plum Village, none of the monks or nuns has a personal bank account, or credit card, or salary, and yet we live very happily. By North American standards, we are not normal at all. But we are very happy to live simply and have a chance to help others and serve the world.

*True happiness depends on our capacity to cultivate
compassion and understanding and bring nourishment
and healing to ourselves and our loved ones.*

All of us need to love and be loved. In our relationships we may look for someone who symbolizes what is good, true, and beautiful, to fill up our own feeling of lack. The person you fall in love with soon becomes the object of your craving. But sexual desire is not the same as love, and sexual relations motivated by craving can never dissipate the feeling of loneliness, but only create more suffering and isolation. If you want to heal your loneliness, you first have to learn how to heal yourself, be there for yourself, and cultivate your own inner garden of love, acceptance, and under-standing.

Once you have cultivated love and understanding in yourself, you have something to offer the other person. But so long as we don't yet love or understand ourselves, how can we blame others for not loving us, or not understanding us? Freedom, peace, love, and understanding are not things we can obtain from the outside. They are something already available within us. Our practice is to do everything we can in order to bring love, understanding, free-dom, and fearlessness to light, by looking deeply into ourselves, and by listening to ourselves. Instead of running after the objects of our craving, or making our loved ones an object of our craving, we should spend the time we have cultivating true love and under-standing in our hearts.

A true friend is someone who offers peace and happiness.
If you're a true friend to yourself, you are able to offer
yourself the true peace and happiness you seek.

I once was asked to write a letter of encouragement to a pris-oner named Daniel, who was on death row in Jackson, Georgia, in the United States. He was nineteen when he committed his crime and had spent thirteen years—his entire adulthood—behind bars. I was asked if I could offer him some words of comfort since the time of his execution was drawing near, and so I sent him a little note. I wrote, "Many people around you have a lot of anger, hate, and despair, which prevents them from getting in touch with the fresh air, the blue sky, or the fragrance of a rose. They are in a kind of prison. But if you practice compassion, if you can see the suffering in the people around you, and if you try to do something to help them suffer less every day, then you will be free. One day with compassion is worth more than one hundred days without it." The number of days we have to live is not so important. What matters is how we live them.

RESTLESSNESS

We all know the feeling of being restless. It is the opposite of feeling at ease and comfortable in ourselves; it's a kind of mental excitement. We cannot be still. We do everything in a hurry, rushing from one thing to the next. Wherever we are, we always think we should be somewhere else. We're even restless in our sleep. No position of the body feels comfortable. We're longing for something and craving something, but we don't know what it is. We open the refrigerator, we check our phone, we pick up a newspaper, we listen to the news—we do everything we can to forget the feeling of loneliness and suffering inside.

We may take refuge in our work, not because we need the money, or because we really want to do it, but because our work distracts us from the painful feelings deep inside. We're rewarded by a sense of achievement in our work, and before we know it, we get addicted to our work. Maybe we turn to films, TV series, the Internet, or computer games, or we listen to music for hours on end. We think these things make us feel better, but as soon as we turn them off, we feel just as bad, if not worse, than we did before. It has become a habit to reach for the phone or computer and immerse ourselves in another world. We do it to survive. But we want to do more than just survive. We want to live.

It is helpful to look honestly at your habit energy. When you turn on the TV, are you sure the program is worth watching? When you reach for some food, is it because you are hungry? What are you running away from? What is it you are really hungry for?

The energy of mindfulness—our spiritual practice body—helps us identify what kind of feeling is coming up and pushing us to run away. Solidly rooted in our mindful breathing, we realize we don't need to run away. We don't need to suppress our painful feelings. We see clearly what is going on inside and take the chance to stop, embrace our feelings, and start to truly take care of ourselves.

Each one of us needs to reconnect with ourselves,
with our loved ones, and with the Earth.

We reconnect with the earth and our cosmic body, which is present in us, supporting us in every moment. We all need deep healing at the roots. Every time we come back to our body with mindful breathing, we put an end to our feelings of isolation and alienation, and we have a chance to heal ourselves completely.

It is possible to learn to sit in peace, breathe in peace, and walk in peace. To be at peace is an art we cultivate with our daily mindfulness practice.

PRACTICE: THE ART OF RELAXATION

In the middle of a difficult day or as soon as you get home, it is possible to create a moment of peace, freedom, and happiness simply by taking a few minutes to come home to your body and relax. This may be something you'd like to try right now. You need only ten to fifteen minutes.

Find a quiet place where you won't be disturbed. Arrange things so your body is in a comfortable position, either sitting or lying down. And then begin to bring your awareness to your whole body. You may like to read one paragraph of the following guidance at a time, and practice it as you go along. Or you can practice with a friend and read the guidance out loud for each other.

First, bring your attention one hundred percent to your breathing, becoming aware of your in-breath as it enters the body and your abdomen rises, and becoming aware of the out-breath as it leaves the body and your abdomen falls. You enjoy following the in-breath and out-breath all the way in and all the way out of your body. You can silently say to yourself the words "rising" and "falling" to help keep your mind focused entirely on your breathing at the level of your abdomen. Following your breathing, you free yourself from your worries and restlessness, and already your body can begin to rest.

We need to train ourselves to keep coming back
to our breath and our body. Every time we reunite
body and mind, we are reconciling with ourselves.

As you breathe in, become aware of your whole body in whatever position it is. As you breathe out, smile to your whole body. It should be a real smile. You may already notice some resistance or tension in your shoulders, chest, arms, or hands. Gently move the body to stretch and release the tension. Still following the breathing, move your head from side to side to relax the neck, or gently stretch your back. You can release any tension that may be there in the chest or abdomen, arms or hands. Allow every part of your body to completely relax.

Breathing in, you feel calm. Breathing out, you feel ease. Smile and allow all the muscles on your face to relax. Gently release the tension from the dozens of muscles in your face.

Start to feel all the areas of your body that are in contact with the floor or the chair: your feet, your heels, the backs of your legs, your bottom, your back, your arms, your legs, your shoulders, and your head. Breathing out, let go of all tension and allow the earth to receive the whole weight of your body. Listen to your body. Embrace your body with loving-kindness, compassion, and care. Send love and healing energy to all your organs and thank them for being there and working in harmony. Send love and gratitude to all the parts of your body. Smile to every cell. Reconnect with your body. Reconcile. "My dear body, I'm sorry I've let you down. I've pushed you too hard. I've been neglecting you. I have allowed stress, tension, and pain to accumulate. Now please allow yourself to rest and relax."

Smile to yourself. Smile to your body. Become aware that the blue sky, white clouds, and stars are above you and all around you. The Earth is holding you in her tender embrace. You are in a state of total rest. You have nothing to do and nowhere to run to. Everything you need is right here in this moment, and you smile.

Relaxation brings happiness, to both your body and your mind. After ten to fifteen minutes of practicing in this way, you will feel rested, refreshed, and ready to continue your day.

MINDFULNESS IS A SOURCE OF HAPPINESS

Are you happy? Are you living a fulfilled life? If you can't touch happiness now, when can you be happy? Happiness is not something you can postpone to the future. You have to challenge yourself to be happy right here and now. If you want to have peace, joy, and happiness, it's only possible to find it in the present moment.

With mindfulness we can learn the art of transforming any moment into a happy moment, a legendary moment. It is the art of arriving in the present moment to recognize all the conditions of happiness we already have. And it is at the same time the art of transforming our suffering. The two go together. Recognizing our conditions of happiness and cultivating moments of happiness help us handle and embrace our suffering. Watering our seeds of joy and well-being helps our suffering transform.

Whether this moment is happy or not depends on you.
It's you who makes the moment happy, not the moment
that makes you happy. With mindfulness, concentration,
and insight, any moment can become a happy moment.

Your quality of life depends on your awareness of all the conditions of happiness that are available to you now. You are alive. You have legs to walk. You have two wonderful eyes; you simply need to open them to enjoy the paradise of colors and forms all around you. Oysters at the bottom of the sea have never seen the bright blue of the sky in daylight or the majesty of the stars at night. They have never seen the ocean waves or heard the sound of the wind or song of the birds. And yet these wonders are available to us. Are you available to them? Mindfulness helps us to arrive in the here and the now and recognize the wonders of life that are right there, within us and around us.

*Happiness is not something that arrives in a package
in the mail. Happiness does not fall out of the sky.
Happiness is something we generate with mindfulness.*

You may like to take a piece of paper and sit somewhere quietly—perhaps in a park, under a tree, or in your favorite spot—and write down all the conditions of happiness you already have. You will soon discover that one page is not enough; even two, three, or four pages are not enough. You may begin to realize you are much luckier than many people. You already have more than enough conditions to be happy, and gratitude and joy naturally arise.

LIVING HAPPILY HERE AND NOW

At the time of the Buddha there was a successful and generous businessman called Anathapindika. He was very loved by his people, and they gave him the name Anathapindika, meaning "the one who helps the destitute."

One day Anathapindika brought several hundred businessmen to hear the Buddha teach. The Buddha taught them that it is possible to live happily right in the here and now. Perhaps he was aware that many businesspeople have a tendency to think a bit too much about success in the future. In his teaching, the Buddha used the expression "living happily in the present moment" five times. He emphasized that we don't have to wait for more conditions of happiness in the future. We don't have to look for success in order to be happy. Life is available only in the present moment, and we already have more than enough conditions to be happy. We can train ourselves to keep bringing our attention back to everything that is going well in the present moment.

The art of dwelling happily in the present moment
is the practice most needed in our time.

BEING NUMBER ONE

Many of us want to be successful. We want to be good in our field. We want to be number one. We tend to think we can be happy only if we're number one. But if you want to be number one, you have to devote all your time and energy to your work. You end up sacrificing quality time with family and friends, and you end up sacrificing time with yourself. Often you even sacrifice your health. In striving to be number one, you end up sacrificing your happiness. What is the point of being number one if you're not happy?

You have to make a choice.
Do you want to be number one,
or do you want to be happy?
You may become a victim of your success,
but you can never become a victim of your happiness.

When you pursue the path of happiness, you are much more likely to be successful in your work. If you are happier and have more inner peace, your work tends to be better. But you have to make happiness your priority. Once you can accept yourself as you are, you allow yourself to be happy. You don't need to become anything or anyone else, just as a rose doesn't need to become a lotus in order to be happy. As a rose, it is already beautiful. You are wonderful just as you are.

EVERY MOMENT IS A DIAMOND

One winter morning in Plum Village I was in my hut getting ready to give a talk. I had ten minutes before the talk was due to start in the meditation hall. Whether ten minutes is a lot or a little depends on how we live them. I put on my long robe and I went into the bathroom to refresh my face. I opened the faucet a little so that only a few drops came out, one by one. As the icy water trickled out, it was as though drops of melted snow were falling into my hand. They were so fresh and cool they woke me up. I lifted up the drops and enjoyed their coolness and freshness on my face. They were like drops of snow from distant Himalayan peaks that had made a long journey of thousands of miles to reach my hut in the woods. And now they landed on my cheeks, my forehead, my eyes. I saw the snow-capped mountain peaks so clearly. Recognizing the presence of the snowflakes in the water, I smiled.

I wasn't thinking about the talk I had to give in a few minutes. I wasn't thinking about anything in the future. I was just dwelling happily in the present moment, experiencing these drops of snow landing gently on my face.

I was all alone in the hut, but I smiled. It wasn't a polite smile—no one was there to see it. I put on my coat and stepped out of the hut to walk to the meditation hall, and I marveled at the sparkling drops of dew on the grass. With every step I took, I was aware that the drops of dew were no different from the drops of snow that I had just put on my face.

Wherever we go, we can encounter Himalayan snowflakes. Whatever we are doing, whether we are washing our face, walking through dewdrops in the morning mist, or looking up at the sky and clouds, we can see the mountain snow is always within us and around us.

We know that about seventy percent of our body is water.
Actually it is seventy percent snow.

We all need a spiritual dimension to our life. With mindfulness we can see the poetry and beauty all around us. We can see the miracles of life. We get deeply in touch with our cosmic body. Every second, every minute, every hour, becomes a diamond.

TIME IS LIFE

When you wake up in the morning, you can choose how you want to start your day. I recommend you start the day smiling. Why smile? Because you are alive and you have twenty-four brand-new hours ahead of you. The new day is a gift of life offered to you. Celebrate it and vow to live it deeply. Vow not to waste it.

Every day is filled with equally miraculous acts—we walk, we breathe, we eat our breakfast and use the bathroom. The art of living is knowing how to generate happiness at any time. No one else can create happiness for us; we have to create it ourselves. With mindfulness and gratitude we can be happy right away.

When you brush your teeth, you can choose to do it in mindfulness. You just focus your attention on brushing your teeth. You may have two or three minutes to brush your teeth and it's possible to transform those two or three minutes into minutes of happiness and freedom. The time of brushing your teeth is not lost time. It is also life. Don't do it just to get it done. Enjoy being mindful, and concentrate on the act of tooth brushing. This is the art of living. You don't need to think of anything else; you don't need to hurry. Just relax and enjoy brushing your teeth. When you do this, you encounter yourself and you encounter life deeply in the present moment.

When I brush my teeth, I enjoy the fact that, even at my age, I still have teeth to brush! Being aware of this is already enough to make me happy. Each one of us can brush our teeth in such a way that makes us happy. And when we go to the toilet, it is also possible to enjoy that time. We are part of the river of life, and we return to the Earth what she has given us. Mindfulness transforms even the most mundane of actions into sacred actions. Any moment can become a meaningful moment where we encounter life deeply—whether we're washing the dishes, washing our hands, or walking to the bus stop.

When you eat, you can cherish every single moment. Mindfulness, concentration, and insight will tell you that this moment of eating is exceptional. It is wonderful to have food to eat.

Every piece of bread and every grain of
rice is a gift of the whole cosmos.

Usually we eat without being aware of what we're eating, because our mind is not present. We are absentminded, the very opposite of being mindful. Often we are not eating our food; we are eating our worries and our projects. Put your thinking aside while you eat and just try to be fully present to taste and enjoy the food and the people around you. Switch off the TV or radio; put aside your phone, the newspaper, or anything else that might distract you. Eating like this, you're not just nourished by the food; you're also nourished by the peace, happiness, and freedom you have while eating.

A PATH OF DISCOVERY

When you are facing a great challenge or difficulty in your life, it may not be easy to get in touch with these simple joys. You may find yourself wondering, "What is the meaning of it all?" You may ask this when you are sick, or when a loved one is sick or passing away, or when you are overwhelmed by despair and life seems to have lost all its meaning.

There is always something we can do to nourish our happiness and take care of ourselves. Even if, in a given moment, we cannot touch deep well-being, perhaps we can increase our happiness by just five or ten percent. That is already something. To meditate is not only to discover the meaning of life, but also to heal and nourish ourselves. As we do so, we have a chance to keep releasing our ideas about what the meaning of life is or isn't.

As we nourish and heal ourselves, our understanding of the meaning of life will deepen day by day.

There is a positive mental formation called "ease"—a relaxed state of peacefulness and tranquillity, like the still water in a calm mountain lake. We cannot be happy, we cannot nourish and heal ourselves, unless we are at ease. The peace of feeling at ease is the most precious thing there is, more precious than any other pursuit.

We all have the capacity to be calm and at ease. But if we haven't been cultivating it, our energy of ease may not yet be very strong. Can you identify those moments when you feel truly at ease? Can you create more of them in your life?

It is possible to breathe in such a way that our in-breath and out-breath are pleasant and peaceful. When we feel joyful, happy, and peaceful as we breathe, we are able to stop running and arrive in the present moment. Healing naturally takes place. But if while breathing we're still trying to attain something, even if that thing is good health or self-control, we haven't yet stopped running. We can allow ourselves to have peace—to *be* at peace.

PRACTICE: THE ART OF SITTING

There is an art to helping your body sit still in such a way that you can feel relaxed and at ease. It may take some training. But it is possible. You *do* have the capacity to experience stillness; you *do* have the capacity to touch peace. Each one of us has a buddha body; we just need to give the buddha in us a chance.

For many of us, when we sit still, we're so restless that it feels as though we're sitting on burning coals. But with some practice, we'll be able to skillfully tame our restless body and mind and sit in peace. As soon as there is ease and relaxation, there is healing and well-being. And wherever we sit, it's as though we're sitting outside on fresh grass in a beautiful spring breeze.

Why do I practice sitting meditation? Because I like it. There's no point doing it if you don't enjoy it. It's not hard labor. Every breath can bring peace, happiness, and freedom. Just sitting down and doing nothing is an art. It's the art of non-doing. You don't have to *do* anything. You don't have to struggle with yourself in order to sit. You don't have to make an effort to be peaceful. Paying attention to the breathing going on is like the sun shining on a flower. The sunshine doesn't try to impose itself on the flower or try to alter the flower in any way. The warmth and energy of the sun penetrates the flower naturally. You can just sit there and enjoy breathing in and breathing out.

You may like to adjust your posture a little, so your back is straight, your legs comfortable, and your shoulders open and relaxed to give enough space for your lungs. Sitting like this allows the breathing to flow naturally and allows our body to relax completely. With relaxation comes healing. Deep healing is not possible without relaxation. You need to learn how to be completely at ease, how to do nothing.

> *Sitting meditation is an act of civilization. These days*
> *we are so busy, we don't even have time to breathe.*
> *To take a moment to sit in stillness and cultivate peace,*
> *joy, and compassion—that is civilization. It is priceless.*

You simply sit there, not doing anything. You are happy to be aware that you are sitting on a very beautiful planet, revolving in a galaxy of stars. You are sitting in the lap of the Earth and over your head there are trillions of stars. If you can sit and see that, what else do you need to sit for? You are in touch with the universe, and your happiness is immense.

CHAPTER 6

LETTING GO
TRANSFORMATION AND HEALING

When we know the art of how to suffer, we suffer much less. We're able to make use of the mud of our suffering to grow lotuses of love and understanding.

Living our life fully and deeply requires courage. If we cannot be happy, right here and right now, we need to ask ourselves why. If we're having difficulty touching peace and the wonders of the cosmos in our daily life, there must be something getting in the way. We need to find out what it is. What's weighing us down or pulling us away from the present moment?

The art of living happily is also the art of transforming our afflictions. If we want to be happy, we need to identify what is preventing us from being happy. The path to well-being is the path out of ill-being. Sometimes we suffer but we don't dare to admit it to ourselves, let alone to others. However, only by facing our suffering can we find the way out, the path to well-being.

A meditator is both an artist and a warrior.

We need to use our creativity and courage to cut through whatever is holding us back from being happy or being free. It's as though we're entangled. We may be entangling ourselves or letting others entangle us. We may even live as though we are saying, "Please tangle me up!" We need both the insight born of meditation and the courage of a warrior to cut through the obstacles on our path and the ropes that entangle us. In the words of the first Zen teacher in Vietnam and China, Master Tang Hoi, "Letting go is the action of heroes."

DISENTANGLING YOURSELF

We may be entangled by our projects, our work, and our fast-paced way of living. We may be caught up in our craving or restlessness. We may be blocked by our sorrow, anger, or fear. We may have been entangled our whole life by the ropes of anger and fear or weighed down by a grudge we can't shake off. A relationship with someone close to us may have become overgrown and buried by weeds of misunderstanding. Or perhaps we are caught up in seeking status, money, or sensual pleasures. All these things prevent us from touching the happiness, peace, and freedom that is available right here in the present moment.

To disentangle ourselves, we need courage and determination. It takes courage to change our livelihood to one that is more in line with our deepest values and aspirations. It takes determination not to get carried away by projects that make us feel stressed and overworked, causing us to neglect ourselves and our loved ones. It takes courage to sit down with our partner, friend, or family member and open up communication.

Each one of us needs to identify our ropes so we can cut ourselves free. We have to make time to sit down and ask ourselves honestly what is entangling us. Wanting to untie the ropes is not enough; we need to understand *why* those ropes entangled us in the first place before we can free ourselves from them.

How long do you have left to live? What is so important that you let it get in the way of your chance to live deeply and happily? When you get your priorities straight, you can let go of the restlessness, frustration, anxiety, and resentment you've been carrying.

Very few people are truly free. We are too busy. Even if we have millions of dollars, even if we are famous and influential, without inner freedom, we can't be truly happy. What we all want most in the world is freedom.

Each one of us has our own idea of happiness. We may think our happiness depends on having a certain job, house, car, or person to live with. Or we may think we have to eliminate this or that from our lives in order to be happy. Some of us think that if only a certain political party was in power, then we'd be happy. But these are just ideas we have created for ourselves. If we let go of our ideas, we can allow ourselves to touch happiness right away. Our *idea* of happiness may be the very *obstacle* standing in the way of our happiness.

LETTING GO

You already have one piece of paper on which you listed all the conditions of happiness you have. Now you need to take another piece of paper, find somewhere quiet to sit, and make a list of everything that is entangling you, everything you need to let go of—including your ideas about happiness. Just naming what you want to release will make you feel lighter. The more you can let go of, the more lightness and freedom you will feel.

Letting go is a source of joy and happiness, but it takes courage. Suppose you live in a busy, polluted city and you want to get away for the weekend. You may say you want to get away, but somehow it never happens because you can't let go of the city. You get entangled in the city so you never see the sweeping hills and the forests, the beach and the mountains, or the moon and the stars. But when a friend finally helps you get away, you begin to feel free as soon as you have left the city behind. You feel the fresh breeze on your face and you see the wide horizon, and you feel better right away. This is the joy of letting go, the joy of leaving your entanglements behind.

TRANSFORMING SUFFERING

Sometimes the obstacle to our happiness is not something we can cut through or let go of easily. A deep feeling of sorrow or despair may establish itself in our hearts, and we need both the fearlessness of a warrior and the skill of an artist to transform it. We can take refuge in our buddha body, our spiritual practice body, and our community body to help us do this.

In 1954, Vietnam—my homeland—was divided into North and South. The war was raging and dragging on and on, with no end in sight. This was when my mother died. It was a very painful, difficult time for me, and I fell into a deep depression. There was nothing the doctors could do. It was only through the practice of mindful breathing and mindful walking that I was finally able to heal.

My experience has shown me that the practice of mindful breathing and mindful walking can help overcome depression, despair, anger, and fear. Every step and every breath can bring healing. If you are depressed, try to practice mindfulness of breathing and walking with all your heart. Even if you do it for just one week, you will be able to transform your suffering and experience relief. Do not give up. Keep coming back to your breathing and walking. Keep trusting in the qualities of fearlessness and perseverance that are there in you. Your seeds of awakening and compassion will help get you through.

When we're facing a personal crisis or suffering from depression, we may feel that life itself is the problem. We may think that if somehow we could throw off this body, then we would not suffer anymore. We want to shed this mortal coil in order to go somewhere where there is no more suffering. But we have seen that this is not possible. Life and death are not what they seem. "To be or not to be: that is [*not*] the question!" There may be birth and death on the level of conventional truth, but on the level of the ultimate truth, to be or not to be is no longer the question. The teachings on emptiness, aimlessness, signlessness, and our eight bodies show us that we are so much more than this body. There is no separate self-entity that can leave this body and go to a place where there is perfect bliss, a place free of suffering.

> *Peace, freedom, and happiness can be found*
> *right here in this very life, if only we can*
> *learn the art of handling our suffering.*

Thanks to having a body and to being alive, we have an opportunity to heal and transform our suffering, and to touch true happiness and the wonders of life. Whatever we can do to heal and transform ourselves is contributing to a more beautiful continuation body not only for us but also for our ancestors.

WHO IS SUFFERING?

When our despair is overwhelming, we need to be able to let go of the idea that our suffering is our own, that this body is our self, and that this body belongs to us. The insight of interbeing and no self will help. Not having a separate self doesn't mean we don't suffer. When conditions for suffering come together, suffering arises. We feel it; we experience it. And when conditions are no longer sufficient, suffering ceases. The good news is that suffering is impermanent. There doesn't need to be a separate self-entity who suffers.

In fact, when our suffering is very great, we can be sure that it is not ours alone. It may have been transmitted to us by our parents, grandparents, or great-grandparents. They may never have had a chance to learn how to transform their pain and suffering, and so this suffering has been passed down for generations. You may be the first one in your family to have encountered teachings and practices that help you recognize and take care of this suffering.

When we are able to transform our suffering,
we do so not only for ourselves but also for
all our ancestors and descendants.

Knowing that you are doing this with them and for them can give you the courage and strength you need to overcome even the most difficult moments. And we know we are cultivating a good continuation body for the future.

Our body is not our own individual property; it is collective. It is the body of our ancestors. In our body we have our mother and father, our nation, our people, our culture, and the whole cosmos.

If we are overwhelmed by despair, we may think that destroying our body will help. But the insight of interbeing shows us that destroying our body would be killing our father, our mother, and our ancestors in us. It is possible to let this suffering, which is not ours alone, pass through the body. It is impermanent. Bit by bit, with fearlessness and perseverance, it can be transformed.

SURVIVING THE STORM

It is possible to use our breathing to embrace our strong emotions and experience relief. We are so vast, and our emotions are just one part of us; we are much more than our emotions. A strong emotion is like a storm that comes, stays a while, and passes. Everyone must learn to survive a storm. The practice of belly breathing is essential. Every time a strong emotion like anger, fear, sadness, or despair comes up, we should go back to our breathing right away so we can take care of the storm raging within us. We are like a tree in a storm. The top branches of the tree may be blowing wildly in the wind, but the trunk and roots are stable and firm. With belly breathing we bring our mind down to our trunk, our abdomen, where it is calm and stable. We should not stay high up in the branches, where we are blown about.

Whether sitting, standing, or lying down, bring your attention to your abdomen and focus one hundred percent on your in- and out-breaths and the rising and falling of the abdomen. Stop thinking about whatever triggered the storm and just follow your breathing, focusing on the belly. After five, ten, or fifteen minutes, the storm of emotion will pass. Your mind will have reestablished its clarity and calm.

Belly breathing is something you can do anytime and anywhere. Whenever you have to sit and wait for a few minutes, instead of reaching for your phone, why not challenge yourself to follow your breathing one hundred percent? This is a way of training your spiritual practice body, and soon bringing your mind to your breathing will become a habitual response that can save you in difficult moments. You can also train to come back to your belly breathing when you encounter smaller difficulties and challenges that arise every day. Then, when the tidal wave of emotion comes, your practice body will be there for you when you need it most.

RECOGNIZING AND EMBRACING SUFFERING

We should not be afraid of suffering. We should be afraid of only one thing, and that is not knowing how to deal with our suffering.

Handling our suffering is an art. If we know how to suffer, we suffer much less, and we're no longer afraid of being overwhelmed by the suffering inside. The energy of mindfulness helps us recognize, acknowledge, and embrace the presence of the suffering, which can already bring some calm and relief.

When a painful feeling comes up, we often try to suppress it. We don't feel comfortable when our suffering surfaces, and we want to push it back down or cover it up. But as a mindfulness practitioner we allow the suffering to surface, so we can clearly identify it and embrace it. This will bring transformation and relief. The first thing we have to do is accept the mud in ourselves. When we recognize and accept our difficult feelings and emotions, we begin to feel more at peace. When we see that mud is something that can help us grow, we become less afraid of it.

When we are suffering, we invite another energy from the depths of our consciousness to come up: the energy of mindfulness. Mindfulness has the capacity to embrace our suffering. It says, "Hello, my dear pain." This is the practice of recognizing suffering. "Hello, my pain. I know you are there, and I will take care of you. You don't need to be afraid."

Now in our mind consciousness there are two energies: the energy of mindfulness and the energy of suffering. The work of mindfulness is first to recognize and then to embrace the suffering with gentleness and compassion. You make use of your mindful breathing to do this. As you breathe in, you say silently, "Hello, my pain." As you breathe out, you say, "I am here for you." Our breathing contains within it the energy of our pain, so as we breathe with gentleness and compassion, we are also embracing our pain with gentleness and compassion.

When suffering comes up, we have to be present for it. We shouldn't run away from it or cover it up with consumption, distraction, or diversion. We should simply recognize it and embrace it, like a mother lovingly embracing a crying baby in her arms. The mother is mindfulness, and the crying baby is suffering. The mother has the energy of gentleness and love. When the baby is embraced by the mother, it feels comforted and immediately suffers less, even though the mother does not yet know exactly what the problem is. Just the fact that the mother is embracing the baby is enough to help the baby suffer less. We don't need to know where the suffering is coming from. We just need to embrace it, and that already brings some relief. As our suffering begins to calm down, we know we will get through it.

When we go home to ourselves with the energy
of mindfulness, we're no longer afraid of being
overwhelmed by the energy of suffering.
Mindfulness gives us the strength to look deeply
and gives rise to understanding and compassion.

Embracing our pain and suffering is an art. It may take some training to learn how to do it. As a meditator, you are an artist, and the art of embracing your suffering is particular to you. You can be creative in how you handle a painful feeling. You may want to draw, paint, listen to inspiring music, or write a poem. Some of my poems that have the most beautiful images were written during the times when I was encountering my greatest suffering. Writing these poems was a way to nourish and comfort myself, so I would not lose my balance and so I would have the strength to continue my work.

When I am experiencing a difficult feeling, I often choose to bring to mind a beautiful, positive memory to comfort me and water the seeds of hope in my consciousness. It may be the memory of my favorite cedar trees in Plum Village or the image of a young child laughing and playing with delight. This is a way to garden the mind. The positive energy of the good seeds gladdens the mind and embraces and penetrates the painful feeling. What would be the positive memories or experiences you could call upon to help embrace and balance the energy of sorrow or despair when it comes up?

It is also possible to take your suffering for a walk, to allow it to be embraced by the earth, the blue sky, the sunshine, and the little miracles of life that are all around you at every moment. To suffer is not enough. You also need to remember that the wonders of life *are* there. When you stay present with your body, present with your breathing, and present with your suffering, you allow Mother Earth and your cosmic body to embrace your pain. You allow the wonders of life to comfort and refresh you and bring you some relief.

A HEALING PRESENCE

When you know how to handle and embrace your own suffering with compassion, you will also know how to help someone else who is experiencing pain, either physically or emotionally. If you have the energies of calm and compassion yourself, then you can be a source of those energies for someone else. When you sit next to them, they can feel the energy of your presence. They can feel your compassion and care. You don't need to do or say anything.

The quality of our presence already changes the situation.

You are just like a tree. You may think that a tree is not doing anything at all, but when you touch a tree or sit at the foot of a tree, you can feel the energy of the tree pervading you. The tree has an energy. It simply stands there, being itself, and that is so refreshing, nourishing, and healing.

Sometimes someone else's suffering can make you feel power-less. It may seem like there is nothing you can do to help them. But in fact, if you can generate and sustain an energy of calm and embrace your own feeling of powerlessness—by following your breathing and relaxing your body—you are taking care of the energy of your tree. Offering a high quality of presence for someone who is suffering can already be very supportive and healing for the other person.

Many of us want to do something to help the world suffer less. We see so much violence, poverty, and environmental destruction all around us. But if we're not peaceful, if we don't have enough compassion, then we can't do much to help. We ourselves are the center. We have to make peace and reduce the suffering in ourselves first, because we represent the world. Peace, compassion, and well-being begin with ourselves. When we can reconcile with ourselves and embrace and transform our suffering, we are also taking care of the world. Don't think that you and the world are two separate things. Anything you do for yourself, you are also doing for the world.

PRACTICE: THE ART OF SUFFERING

If you want to understand your suffering, you first need to calm yourself down. You need to embrace your suffering with compassion. Then you have a chance to look deeply into it, in order to understand its roots and transform it.

Don't Run Away

We know there's suffering within us, but we don't want to go home and listen to it. We're afraid we'll be overwhelmed by the pain, the sorrow, and the despair inside, so we try to run away from ourselves and suppress it. But as long as we run away, we'll never have a chance to heal and transform. So the first step in the art of suffering is to use the energy of mindfulness to be present for your suffering. Your spiritual practice body—your mindful breathing and the energy of mindfulness, concentration, and insight—gives you the courage and stability to recognize, handle, and embrace what's coming up.

Avoid the Second Arrow

Someone who is hit by an arrow is in a great deal of pain, but if a second arrow comes along and hits that person in the same place, the pain will be ten times worse. Your suffering is the first arrow. And the second arrow is your irritation, anger, resistance, and re-

THE ART OF LIVING

action to whatever is coming up. The second arrow could be your fear, which imagines the situation to be much worse than it is; it could be your inability to accept that you are suffering, or it could be your frustration or regrets. You have to be calm and recognize your suffering clearly, just as it is, without exaggerating or amplifying it with other worries.

Identify the Roots

When you embrace your suffering with mindfulness, you discover that your suffering carries within it the suffering of your father, your mother, and your ancestors, as well as the suffering of your people, your nation, and the world. Many of us may have experienced moments of acute sadness, fear, or despair that we don't understand. We don't know where the feelings come from. When you look deeply enough, you are able to see the deep roots that may be ancestral suffering passed down to you. This helps you transform the suffering, reducing the pain and despair you feel.

Nothing can survive without food. This is just as true for suffering as it is for love. If your suffering, sorrow, or depression has been going on for some time, there must be something that is feeding it. Every day we are consuming our thoughts, we are consuming TV, movies, music, conversations, and even the collective consciousness and environment around us, which may be toxic. So be attentive and reflect deeply to see whether these elements are feeding your suffering at the roots. As we start to change our habits of thinking, speaking, behaving, and consuming, we cut off and uproot these sources of food, and our suffering will steadily begin to die. As it dies it becomes compost, nourishing new flowers of understanding and compassion in the garden of our heart.

THE GOODNESS OF SUFFERING

It's very tempting to want to stay strong and healthy and never suffer any pain or illness. Many of us hope we will never have to encounter serious difficulties or challenges in our lives. But my own experience is that had I not encountered great difficulties and suffering, I would never have had a chance to grow on my spiritual path; I would never have had the chance to heal, transform, and touch such profound peace, joy, and freedom. If we don't experience suffering, how can we ever generate understanding and compassion? Compassion is born from understanding suffering, and without understanding and compassion, we cannot be a happy person.

I care very deeply for my students, but I would never want to send them to a heaven or any place where there was no suffering. We cannot create happiness in a place where there is no suffering, just as we cannot grow lotuses without mud. Happiness and peace are born from transforming suffering and pain. If there was no mud, how could a lotus grow? Lotuses cannot grow on marble.

CHAPTER 7

NIRVANA IS NOW

Nirvana is a pleasant state of coolness and
freshness that we can all touch in this very life.

By using mindfulness, concentration, and insight to transform our suffering, we can touch nirvana in the here and now. Nirvana is not some distant place in a distant future.

"Nirvana" is a word that comes from an ancient rural dialect of India. In the Buddha's time, as in many places around the world today, rural families would cook over a small fire made from straw, dung, wood, or even rice husks. Every morning, the first thing the mother would do is light the fire to prepare breakfast for family members going out to work in the fields. She would hold her hand above the ashes from the night before, to see if they were still warm. If they were, she would only need to add some straw or twigs to rekindle the fire. But if the fire had gone out, she would find that the ashes were completely cold. After a fire has completely gone out, if you sink your hands into the ashes, it feels pleasantly cool.

The Buddha used the word "nirvana" to describe the pleasant experience of the cooling of the flames of our afflictions. Many of us are burning in the fire of our craving, fear, anxiety, despair, or regret. Our anger or jealousy, or even our ideas about death and loss, can burn us up inside. But when we transform our suffering and remove our wrong ideas, very naturally, we can touch a refreshing peace. This is nirvana.

There is an intimate connection between our suffering and nirvana. If we did not suffer, how could we recognize the peace of nirvana? Without suffering, there can be no awakening from suffering, just as without the hot coals, we cannot have the cool ashes. Suffering and awakening go together.

> *As we learn to handle our suffering,*
> *we are learning to generate moments of nirvana.*

Nirvana does not have to be something big, something we spend a lifetime practicing for, hoping to one day experience. Each one of us can touch small moments of nirvana every day. Suppose you're walking barefoot and you accidentally step on a briar, and a dozen thorns pierce your foot. Immediately you lose all peace and happiness. But as soon as you're able to remove one thorn, and then another, you begin to get some relief—you get some nirvana. And the more thorns you remove, the greater the relief and peace. In the same way, the removal of afflictions *is* the presence of nirvana. As you recognize, embrace, and transform your anger, fear, and despair, you start to experience nirvana.

TOUCHING NIRVANA

The Buddha taught that we can enjoy nirvana with our very body. We *need* our body—we need our feelings, perceptions, mental formations, and consciousness—in order to touch nirvana. We can touch it with our feet, our eyes, our hands. It is thanks to being alive with our human body that we can experience the cooling of the flames and generate moments of nirvana.

When we cool the flames of our anger and, having understood its roots, the anger transforms into compassion, this is the experience of nirvana. When we experience the peace and freedom of walking meditation, we are touching our cosmic body; we are touching nirvana. When we stop running, let go of all our worries about the future and regrets about the past, and come back to enjoy the wonders of life in the present moment, that is when we touch nirvana.

It is by getting in touch deeply with the historical dimension in the present moment that we can touch the ultimate. The two do not exist separately. As we touch our cosmic body, the world of phenomena, we get in touch with the ultimate: the realm of reality-in-itself.

When we see the world of phenomena from the perspective of the ultimate, we see that if there were no death, there could not be birth. If there were no suffering, there could not be happiness. Without mud, there could be no lotus. They depend on each other to manifest. Birth and death are just ideas at the level of the historical dimension. They are not the true nature of reality in the ultimate dimension, which transcends all ideas and notions, all signs and appearances. In the ultimate dimension of reality-in-itself, there is no birth and no death, no suffering and no happiness, no coming and no going, no good and no evil. When we can let go of all ideas and notions—including the ideas of a "self," a "human being," a "living being," or a "life span"—we touch the true nature of reality in itself; we touch nirvana.

Nirvana is the ultimate dimension. It is the extinction and letting go of all notions and ideas. The concentrations on emptiness, signlessness, aimlessness, impermanence, non-craving, and letting go all help us get a breakthrough into the true nature of reality. By contemplating deeply our physical body and the realm of phenomena, we get in touch with nirvana—the true nature of the cosmos, our God body—and we experience peace, happiness, and the freedom of non-fear. We are no longer afraid of birth and death, being and nonbeing.

Just as birds enjoy soaring in the sky, and deer enjoy roaming in the woods, so do the wise ones enjoy dwelling in nirvana. We don't have to look very far to find nirvana, because it is our true nature in this very moment. You cannot remove the ultimate from yourself.

To touch nirvana is to realize the insight of
no birth and no death in our daily life.

NIRVANA IS NOT ETERNAL DEATH

Many people mistakenly think that nirvana describes a blissful state or a place we enter after we die. We may have heard it said that "the Buddha entered nirvana after he died." It sounds like nirvana is a place we go to after death. But this is very misleading, and it can give rise to many dangerous misunderstandings. It suggests we cannot touch nirvana when we are alive; we have to die in order to get there. But this is not at all what the Buddha taught.

Once I was on a teaching tour in Malaysia. As we drove through Kuala Lumpur we saw billboards advertising a Buddhist funeral service company calling itself Nirvana. I thought it was very unkind to the Buddha to identify nirvana with death like that. The Buddha never identified nirvana with death. Nirvana is associated with life in the here and now. One of the greatest misunderstandings of Western Buddhist scholars has been to define nirvana as a kind of "eternal death" that ends the cycle of reincarnation. This is a grave misunderstanding of the deepest meaning of nirvana. Why would millions of people follow a religion that teaches eternal death? The very idea of eternal death is still caught in notions of being and nonbeing, birth and death, but the true nature of reality transcends all these notions. It is only when we are alive that we can touch nirvana. I hope someone in Kuala Lumpur might be able to convince that funeral company to change its name.

THE ONE REALITY OF INTERBEING

With the insight of interbeing, we have seen how nothing in the world, including our bodies, exists by itself, alone. All things are mutually dependent on one another. If things were never dirty, how could they be immaculate? Without suffering, there could never be happiness, and without evil, there could never be goodness. If there were not suffering, how could we look deeply into it to give rise to understanding and love? Without suffering, how could there be insight? If there were no wrong, how could we know what right is?

We say, "God is good; God is love," but if God is good and if God is love, does this mean God is not in those places where there is no goodness and love? This is a very big question. In the light of Buddhist teachings, we can say that the ultimate nature of reality, the true nature of God, transcends all notions, including the notions of good and evil. To say anything less is to diminish God.

In the face of devastating natural disasters in which thousands of people die, there are those who ask, "How can God, who is good, allow such suffering?"

When we hear news of wars, terrorist attacks, natural disasters, earthquakes, tsunamis, or hurricanes, we may feel overwhelmed by despair. It is hard to make sense of it. We don't understand why some of us have to endure such suffering and death, but not others. The insight of emptiness can help. When a young baby, an elderly grandmother, a teenager, or a young man dies in a disaster, we feel somehow that a part of us also dies. We die with them because we don't have a separate self, we all belong to the same human species. Insofar as we are still alive, they are also still alive in us. When we can touch this insight of no self, we are inspired to live in a such a way that they continue, beautifully, in us.

Nirvana, the ultimate nature of reality, is indeterminate; it is neutral. That is why everything in the cosmos is a wonder. The lotus is a wonder, and so too is the mud. The magnolia is a wonder, and so too is the poison oak. Ideas of good and evil are created by our mind, not by nature. When we let go of and release all these ideas, we see the true nature of reality. We cannot call an earthquake, storm, or volcano "good" or "evil." Everything has its role to play.

So we may need to reexamine our way of seeing God. If God is only on the side of goodness, then God cannot be the ultimate reality. We cannot even say that God is the ground of all being, because if God is the ground of being, what is the ground of nonbeing? We cannot speak of God in terms of existing or not existing, being or nonbeing. Even the peace and happiness that arises from touching the ultimate comes from within us, not from the ultimate itself. The ultimate, nirvana, is not *itself* peace or joy, because no notion or category like "peace" or "goodness" can be applied to the ultimate. The ultimate transcends all categories.

DON'T WAIT FOR NIRVANA

When the Buddha attained enlightenment at the foot of the Bodhi tree, he was a human being, and after his enlightenment, he was still a human being, with all the suffering and afflictions that having a human body entails. The Buddha was not made of stone. He experienced feelings and emotions, pain, cold, hunger, and fatigue, just like all of us. We shouldn't think that because we experience the suffering and afflictions of being human, we cannot touch peace, we cannot touch nirvana. Even after his enlightenment, the Buddha experienced suffering. From his teachings and stories about his life, we know that he suffered. But the key point is that he knew how to suffer. His awakening came from suffering: he knew how to make good use of his afflictions in order to experience awakening. And because of this, he suffered much less than most of us.

One breath or one step taken in mindfulness can already bring us real happiness and freedom. But as soon as we stop practicing, suffering manifests. Small moments of peace, happiness, and freedom steadily come together to create great awakening and great freedom. What more can we ask for? And yet many of us still think that as soon as we experience awakening, that's it, we're enlightened! We think that after that, we'll have no more problems; we can say goodbye to suffering forever. But that's not possible. Awakening and suffering always go together. Without the one, we can't have the other. If we run away from our suffering, we will never be able to find awakening. So it's okay to suffer—we just need to learn how to handle it. Awakening can be found right in the heart of our suffering. It is thanks to transforming the heat of the fire that we can touch the coolness of nirvana. The practices in this book can help you touch peace and freedom at every step along the path.

TIME TO LIVE

The seven concentrations on emptiness, signlessness, aimlessness, impermanence, non-craving, letting go, and nirvana are very practical. As we apply them in our daily life, we experience increasing freedom from fear, anxiety, anger, and despair. The insight of interbeing and interdependence helps us enjoy the present moment more fully, recognizing the vastness of our being and cherishing all our different bodies. We are able to live true to ourselves, reconcile with our loved ones, and transform our difficulties and suffering.

With the insight of these concentrations, our life begins to acquire a deeper quality. There's more joy, peace, and compassion in whatever we do. We realize that we don't have to wait to go to heaven or nirvana to be happy; we can touch heaven and nirvana right here on Earth. When we touch reality deeply in the present moment, we touch eternity. We transcend birth and death, being and nonbeing, coming and going. We master the art of living, and we know we're not wasting our life. We don't just want to live. We want to live well.

The immediate product of your practice of mindfulness is joy, solidity, and happiness in every moment. Suppose you are walking mindfully from the parking lot to your office. Every step is peace. Every step is freedom. Every step is healing. Arriving at your office is only a by-product. By learning to walk in freedom like that, you develop the habit of dwelling happily in the present moment. The freedom and happiness of the walking enters every cell of your body. If you can do this every day, then walking mindfully will become a way of life—an art of living—that you can transmit to your children.

Scientists tell us that to live is to learn. For millions of years our species has been learning. We have been learning to adapt to our environment. We have been learning in order to survive. With natural selection, those who can't adapt don't survive. If we want to survive in our fast-paced society that is overwhelmed by stress, anxiety, fear, and despair, we have to learn how to deal with it. And what we learn becomes part of our genetic and spiritual heritage that we transmit to future generations. That heritage is in our cells and in our collective consciousness.

Human beings evolved from *Homo habilis* to *Homo erectus* before we became *Homo sapiens,* and every new stage in our evolution came about as a result of learning. Some people have spoken of the new species called *Homo conscius,* humans with the capacity of being mindful. The Buddha belonged to this species. His disciples, and disciples of these disciples, also belong to this species. They have learned how to do things with awareness. They walk mindfully, they eat mindfully, they work mindfully. They have learned that with mindfulness there is concentration and insight—the kind of insight that enables them to live their lives more deeply and avoid danger. And by living, they learn.

If a species can't adapt, it won't survive. There are two ways to adapt to the current situation. The first is to find ways to protect yourself in situations of danger, stress, or despair, so that instead of being a victim of your environment, you can survive. Your daily practice is a way of protecting yourself. The way you think, the way you breathe, the way you walk are kinds of protection. Thanks to the energy of mindfulness, concentration, and insight, you can survive in a stressful, toxic environment, and thanks to your understanding and compassion, you don't contribute to making it any worse. As a member of the *Homo conscius* species, the fruit of your learning will be inscribed in every cell of your body and be transmitted to future generations. Future generations in turn will profit from your experience, so they will not only be able to survive challenging situations but also be able to lead happy and fulfilled lives.

As a monk, I do not have genetic children or grandchildren, but I do have spiritual children. I have seen that it is possible to transmit my realization and wisdom, and the capacity to adapt, to my students—my spiritual children and grandchildren. Just as I look like my parents, so do my students and disciples also somehow look like me. This is not genetic transmission, but spiritual transmission. There are many thousands of people in the world who walk, sit, smile, and breathe like me. This is proof of a real transmission that has been incorporated into the life of my students and inscribed in every cell of their bodies. Later on, my students will in turn transmit this adaptation to their descendants.

We can all contribute to helping *Homo conscius*—the species that embodies mindfulness, compassion, and enlightenment—develop and continue in the world for a long time. The world is in great need of enlightenment, understanding, compassion, mindfulness, and concentration. There is so much suffering caused by stress, depression, violence, discrimination, and despair, and we need a spiritual practice. With a spiritual practice, we will be able to adapt and survive. By living with solidity and freedom, we can transmit mindfulness, concentration, insight, joy, and compassion to others. This is our legacy, our continuation body, and we hope future generations will inherit our life's offering.

But suppose you adapt in a different way. Seeing everyone around you so busy, you try to be even busier in order to keep up. Others have tactics to get to the top, so you adopt those same tactics to be number one—in your work and in your social environment. You might be successful for a time, but in the end, this adaptation is self-destructive, for you as an individual and for the species as a whole.

In today's society we are so busy we don't even have time to take care of ourselves. We're not at ease with ourselves. We find it difficult to take care of our body, feelings, and emotions. We're afraid of being overwhelmed by our suffering, and so we run away from ourselves. This is one of the defining characteristics of our civilization.

But if we run away from ourselves, how can we take care of all our pain? If we can't take care of ourselves, how can we take care of the people we love? And how can we take care of Mother Earth? Mother Earth has the capacity to nourish and heal us, but we are running away from her and even causing her harm and destruction. Technology is allowing us to become ever more adept at running away from ourselves, from our family, and from nature.

There needs to be a revolution, a kind of gentle revolution, a kind of awakening, in each one of us. We need to rebel. We need to declare, "I don't want to continue like this! This is not a life. I don't have enough time to live. I don't have enough time to love."

Once we've started a revolution in our own consciousness, it will bring about radical change in our family and community. But first we need to be determined to change our way of living. We need to reclaim our freedom to enjoy the wonders of life. When we're happy, we'll have the energy and strength we need to help others do the same.

When we stop to breathe, we're not wasting time. Western capitalist civilization says "Time is money" and that we should use our time to make money. We can't afford to stop and breathe or enjoy a walk or marvel at the setting sun. We cannot afford to lose time. But time is more precious than money. Time is life. Coming back to our breathing and becoming aware that we have a wonderful body—this is life.

Do you have time to enjoy the glorious sunrise? Do you have time to enjoy the music of the falling rain, the birds singing in the trees, or the gentle sound of the rising tide? We need to wake up from a long dream. It *is* possible to live differently. Can you see that you already want to live differently?

Time is not money. Time is life, and time is love.

With collective awakening, things can change very quickly. That is why everything we do should be directed toward bringing about collective awakening. Humans can be hateful, mean, and violent, but we also have the ability, with spiritual practice, to become compassionate and protective toward not only our own species but other species too—the ability to be awakened beings who can protect our planet and preserve her beauty. Awakening is our hope. And awakening is possible.

We need to shake ourselves awake so we can change our way of living, so we can have more freedom, more happiness, more vitality, more compassion, more love. We have to reorganize our life so we have time to take care of our body, our feelings, our emotions, our loved ones, and our planet. Taking care of ourselves and others is the kind of adaptation we want to pass on to future generations. We have to remove the pressures that society puts on us. We have to resist. Simply our way of walking from the parking lot to our office is a way of reacting: "I refuse to run. I resist. I will not lose a single moment or a single step. I reclaim my freedom, peace, and joy with every step. This is my life, and I want to live it deeply."

A PATH OF HAPPINESS

The five mindfulness trainings represent the Buddhist vision for a global spirituality and ethic. They are nonsectarian and their nature is universal. All spiritual traditions have their equivalent to these trainings, which are not commandments but practices of compassion born from mindfulness and insight.

They are a way of living that embodies the insight of interbeing—the insight that everything is connected to everything else and that happiness and suffering are not an individual matter. Following the five mindfulness trainings is a concrete way to apply the insights of contemplating emptiness, signlessness, aimlessness, impermanence, non-craving, letting go, and nirvana in our daily life. They express the art of living mindfully—a way of living that can help us transform and heal ourselves, our family, our society, and the Earth. They help us cultivate the best kind of adaptation that we want to pass on to future generations. The trainings are a path of happiness, and by simply knowing we are on the path, we can touch peace, happiness, and freedom every step along the way.

THE FIVE MINDFULNESS TRAININGS

1. Reverence for Life

Aware of the suffering caused by the destruction of life, I am committed to cultivating the insight of interbeing and compassion, and learning ways to protect the lives of people, animals, plants, and minerals. I am determined not to kill, not to let others kill, and not to support any act of killing in the world, in my thinking, or in my way of life. Seeing that harmful actions arise from anger, fear, greed, and intolerance, which in turn come from dualistic and discriminative thinking, I will cultivate openness, non-discrimination, and non-attachment to views in order to transform violence, fanaticism, and dogmatism in myself and in the world.

2. True Happiness

Aware of the suffering caused by exploitation, social injustice, stealing, and oppression, I am committed to practicing generosity in my thinking, speaking, and acting. I am determined not to steal and not to possess anything that should belong to others; and I will share my time, energy, and material resources with those who are in need. I will practice looking deeply to see that the happiness and suffering of others are not separate from my own happiness and suffering; that true happiness is not possible without understanding and compassion; and that running after wealth, fame, power, and sensual pleasures can bring much suffering and despair. I am aware that happiness depends on my mental attitude, not on external conditions, and that I can live happily in the present moment simply by remembering that I already have more than enough conditions to be happy. I am committed to practicing Right Livelihood so that I can help reduce the suffering of living beings on Earth and reverse the process of global warming.

3. True Love

Aware of the suffering caused by sexual misconduct, I am committed to cultivating responsibility and learning ways to protect the safety and integrity of individuals, couples, families, and society. Knowing that sexual desire is not love, and that sexual activity motivated by craving always harms myself as well as others, I am determined not to engage in sexual relations without true love and a deep, long-term commitment made known to my family and friends. I will do everything in my power to protect children from sexual abuse and to prevent couples and families from being broken by sexual misconduct. Seeing that body and mind are one, I am committed to learning appropriate ways to take care of my sexual energy and to cultivating loving-kindness, compassion, joy, and inclusiveness—which are the four basic elements of true love—for my greater happiness and the greater happiness of others. Practicing true love, we know that we will continue beautifully into the future.

4. Loving Speech and Deep Listening

Aware of the suffering caused by unmindful speech and the inability to listen to others, I am committed to cultivating loving speech and compassionate listening in order to relieve suffering and to promote reconciliation and peace in myself and among other people, ethnic and religious groups, and nations. Knowing that words can create happiness or suffering, I am committed to speaking truthfully, using words that inspire confidence, joy, and hope. When anger is manifesting in me, I am determined not to speak. I will practice mindful breathing and walking in order to recognize and to look deeply into my anger. I know that the roots of anger can be found in my wrong perceptions and lack of understanding of the suffering in myself and in the other person. I will speak and listen in a way that can help me and the other person to transform suffering and see the way out of difficult situations. I am determined not to spread news that I do not know to be certain and not to utter words that can cause division or discord. I will practice Right Diligence to nourish my capacity for understanding, love, joy, and inclusiveness, and gradually transform anger, violence, and fear that lie deep in my consciousness.

5. Nourishment and Healing

Aware of the suffering caused by unmindful consumption, I am committed to cultivating good health, both physical and mental, for myself, my family, and my society by practicing mindful eating, drinking, and consuming. I will practice looking deeply into how I consume the Four Kinds of Nutriments, namely edible foods, sense impressions, volition, and consciousness. I am determined not to gamble, or to use alcohol, drugs, or any other products that contain toxins, such as certain websites, electronic games, TV programs, films, magazines, books, and conversations. I will practice coming back to the present moment to be in touch with the refreshing, healing, and nourishing elements in me and around me, not letting regrets and sorrow drag me back into the past nor letting anxieties, fear, or craving pull me out of the present moment. I am determined not to try to cover up loneliness, anxiety, or other suffering by losing myself in consumption. I will contemplate interbeing and consume in a way that preserves peace, joy, and well-being in my body and consciousness, and in the collective body and consciousness of my family, my society, and the earth.

Zen master Thich Nhat Hanh was a global spiritual leader, poet, and peace activist, revered throughout the world for his powerful teachings and bestselling writings on mindfulness and peace. His key teaching is that through mindfulness, we can learn to live happily in the present moment—the only way to truly develop peace, both in one's self and in the world. Thich Nhat Hanh was a pioneer in bringing Buddhism to the West, founding six monasteries and dozens of practice centers in America and Europe as well as more than a thousand local mindfulness practice communities, known as sanghas. He built a thriving community of more than six hundred monks and nuns worldwide, who, together with his tens of thousands of lay students, apply his teachings on mindfulness, peacemaking, and community building in schools, workplaces, businesses, and even prisons throughout the world. Thich Nhat Hanh was a gentle, humble monk—the man Dr. Martin Luther King Jr. called "an apostle of peace and nonviolence."

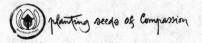 *planting seeds of Compassion*

THANK YOU for supporting Thich Nhat Hanh through the purchase of this book. Sadly, books only provide part of the necessary funds for Thich Nhat Hanh and his 600 monks and nuns to spread teachings of peace, mindfulness and compassion around the world.

If this book was helpful to you, please consider joining the Thich Nhat Hanh Continuation Fund today.

You'll join many others who want to share these life-changing messages of compassion and peace. Your monthly gift will help more people discover the practices of mindfulness, loving speech, and deep listening that can help reduce suffering throughout the world.

To join today, make a one-time gift or learn more, please go to: www.ThichNhatHanhFoundation.org/giving.

Please consider how Thich Nhat Hanh's teachings have affected you personally. Your gift will help bring this wisdom and compassion to many more people and ease their suffering.

Thich Nhat Hanh Continuation and Legacy Foundation
2499 Melru Lane, Escondido, CA USA 92026
www.ThichNhatHanhFoundation.org
info@ThichNhatHanhFoundation.org